Magnificent Motorcycle Trips of the World

38 Guided Tours from 6 Continents

Colette Coleman
with a foreword by Ted Simon

COMPANIONHOUSE™
BOOKS

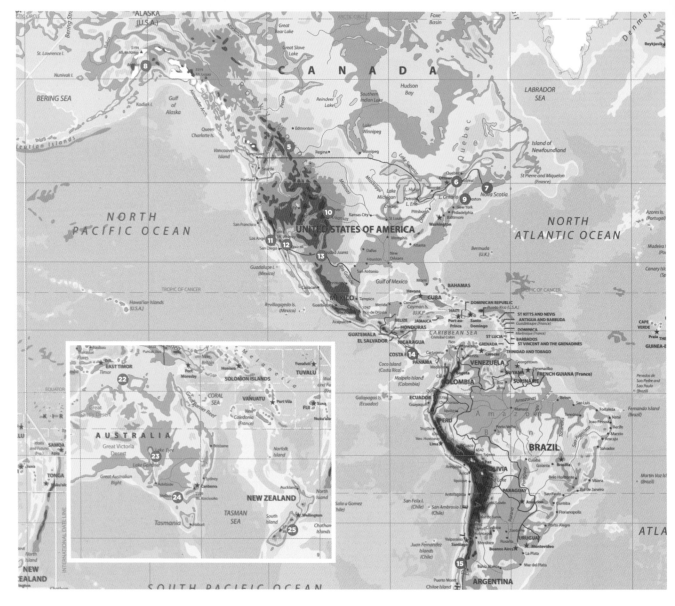

CONTENTS

Foreword 4

Introduction 6

Africa 14

1 Morocco Ceuta to Marrakech Loop 16

2 Kenya Nairobi to the Central Highlands and the Great Rift Valley....................22

3 Namibia Windhoek to Etosha National Park 28

4 South Africa Cape Town Circuit through the Garden Route..............................32

The Americas 38

5 Canada The Rockies: Calgary to Jasper 40

6 Canada Montréal to the Gaspé Peninsula 44

7 Canada The Gulf of Maine to the Strait of Belle Isle 48

8 USA/Canada Alaska: Anchorage to Whitehorse Loop 52

9 USA Boston to the Green Mountains 58

10 USA Denver to Durango via the Black Hills of South Dakota...........................62

11 USA The Wild West and the Californian Coast 70

12 USA Route 66: Flagstaff to Los Angeles 76

13 Mexico The Sierra Madre Mountains to the Baja Peninsula 80

14 Costa Rica San José to Cordillera de Guanacaste 86

15 Chile/Argentina Patagonia: Journey to the End of the World 92

Asia 98

16 Sri Lanka Colombo Circuit 100

17 India Delhi to Jaisalmer...106

18 India Manali to Leh 112

19 Thailand Chiang Mai to Golden Triangle Loop 116

20 Vietnam A Circuit North from Hanoi 120

21 Mongolia Ulaanbaatar to Gobi Desert Loop 124

Australasia 128

22 **Australia** Darwin to Alice Springs: the Top End to the Red Centre......................130

23 **Australia** The Oodnadatta Track 134

24 **Australia** The Great Ocean Road 138

25 **New Zealand** South Island Circuit 142

Europe 146

26 **Iceland** The Ring Road Tour 148

27 **Norway** Fjordland to the North Cape 152

28 **Scotland** Edinburgh to Gairloch in the Northwest Highlands............................156

29 **Ireland** Cork to the Cliffs of Moher 162

30 **England** Kendal to Whitby 166

31 **Germany** Rhineland Wine Trails and the Nürburgring..172

32 **France** Annecy Circuit via the Côte d'Azur..176

33 **Spain/France** Bilbao to Perpignan Loop 180

34 **Spain** A Circuit of Andalucía 184

35 **Switzerland/Austria** The Swiss Alps to the Austrian Tyrol..................................188

36 **Italy** The Dolomites..192

37 **Slovenia/Croatia** The Julian Alps to the Opatija Riviera 196

38 **Turkey** Istanbul Loop via Anatolia and the Coast..200

Index 206

Photo Credits 207

About the Author 208

Acknowledgments 208

FOREWORD BY TED SIMON

There are so many ways to make discoveries in this world. With a good eye, and in the right frame of mind, even a walk to the office can be an adventure, because journeys, I have always insisted, are made in the imagination. But there is no doubt that the further you go, the more there is for the imagination to feed on.

When I started traveling, as an adolescent immediately after the Second World War, everywhere outside Britain was unknown to me. My first trip, alone by bicycle across an exhausted and war-ravaged France, was as thrilling and demanding as anything I've done since. That wonderful experience lured me back, time and again, to various parts of southern Europe, usually by train or by car, and I became addicted. Like most people, I was limited to a few vacation weeks, but I learned how to pack an immense amount into a short time.

Then, in the sixties, I was able for the first time to leave on a journey with no prescribed end in sight. The effect of being able simply to go wherever the wind blew me was quite magical; remarkable opportunities seemed to burst upon me around every corner, and a dazzling sense of liberation made it impossible to go back to a life of office routine. I realized that I was drawn relentlessly to the Mediterranean, and eventually I found a way to live alongside it.

That was just the first time that travel changed my life, but I had still not discovered the motorcycle. Only when I became determined to see the rest of the world did I wake up to the fact that the motorbike really was the perfect vehicle to do this on, and since then I have rarely traveled by any other means. There are so many different degrees of pleasure to be had on a bike; everything from gentle meanderings among the civilized orchards and meadows of Europe, to the wild isolation of the Altiplano in South America. There is something for everyone in the world, just as there is in this book.

Planning a journey can be as much fun as the journey itself. The excitement of trying to picture places and people one has never seen, of trying to anticipate unforeseeable pleasures and problems, of trying to imagine how one will react in a dire situation – these thoughts can make the adrenaline pump. If the journey is a long one through unfamiliar territory, it is hard to stop the imagination from working overtime, especially if you expect to ride solo. When I contemplated the journey I had set for myself in 1973, I

was sometimes overwhelmed by anxiety about my complete ignorance of the countries and cultures I intended to pass through.

I remember so vividly laying out the three Michelin maps that cover Africa on the living room floor, and being astounded by its vastness. How could I have the temerity to think I would survive all this? But, as someone once said, there are no foreign places, only foreign visitors. I calmed myself by remembering that wherever I went, however exotic it might seem to me, for the people who lived there it was humdrum normality. They survived there from day to day, so why shouldn't I? And once I got going, the immensity of the journey evaporated, and every new day became its own adventure.

Now that I have seen so much, it's easy to forget what a huge rush it can be to wander out into the unknown world, even if what's unknown may lie a relatively short distance away. Anywhere can contain an adventure – even coming back from the Andes and the Himalayas, I was amazed to see just how impressive the European Alps were.

There is so much more to be said, about bikes, equipment, choices (traveling alone or in company), risks, and timing, but every rider is different, every journey is unique, and the joy of it is that you can't possibly know what will happen down the road. The important thing is to go, and what better place to start planning your journey than in the pages of this book.

Off-road biking in South Africa.

"I travel not to go anywhere,
but to go. I travel for travel's sake.
The great affair is to move."
~Robert Louis Stevenson

WHY A MOTORCYCLE?

For me, this oft-quoted line sums up completely the joys of travel by motorcycle – whether it is a short ride from home on a crisp, clear morning or a year-long adventure to the other side of the world. The memories that you bring home are of the riding: those days when you and your machine flowed as you wound your way over high passes; or the days when even a few miles seemed to take hours – but the huge sense of achievement as you wearily unpacked your bike at the end of a hard day's ride made you leap out of bed the next day to do it again. It is the riding that you remember the most, the incredible views you saw from the seat of your bike, and the people you met on the journey. Traveling by motorcycle is a wonderful way of meeting people, inspiring interest and passion. Children love motorcycles, fellow riders will stop to chat, and for the people you meet on your journey it is a conversation opener – a means of engaging with a complete stranger. Motorcycles are a necessary form of transport in many countries. Many people own one, so there is instantly a connection, a shared interest. Motorcycling is also a wonderfully solitary experience, almost a form of mechanical meditation, and yet on your bike you never feel alone.

On a motorcycle you really do feel part of the landscape, completely open to the elements, the noise and the surface of the road. It is only on a bike that you can smell Australian roadkill from a distance of 10 miles (16km), or ride through a busy bazaar and catch the aroma of your lunch before you see it. You can park your motorcycle anywhere – a hotel lobby, or even in your room. If you need to cross countries, vast distances, or find yourself at a closed border, there is always the option to transport your bike by sea, air, or train.

Many people dream of traveling by motorcycle, but concerns about their own ability or lack of mechanical knowledge can stop them from taking it any further. You don't have to be an experienced rider or be able to rebuild

Capitol Reef National Park, USA.

an engine by the side of the road. You set your own pace and, if there are problems with your bike, you'll always be able to find someone to help. As for dropping your motorcycle – well, if you intend riding on any of Australia's fantastic dirt roads, chances are that you probably will. It isn't a big issue. I've yet to own a bike I can pick up, but I've never had a problem finding someone to help. Once you are out there, these issues, if they arise, usually result in newfound friends and a reminder of the kindness of strangers.

The Journeys

The thinking behind this book is that motorcycle travel is so much easier these days, and that any of the featured journeys can be taken as part of an average two- to three-week vacation, a short break taken in your own country, or possibly even a few days out of a family vacation. If you have a little longer, then many of the featured journeys can be linked. It is not necessary to pack up all your possessions, give up your job, and take a year out to experience riding in some of the world's most remote regions, but I would definitely recommend it if you can!

The featured journeys are not a definitive list of the world's best motorcycle trips, but a small selection of journeys that are currently accessible to most nationalities. I have chosen countries where bike hire is available or where there are options to pick up a bike as part of an organized tour. I have included some of the world's classic motorcycle journeys, but also many countries that may not immediately spring to mind when planning a motorcycle trip. I have also tried to include a range of riding terrain. Some countries, such as Morocco, lend themselves to both tarmac and off-road trips.

above left: The lure of the open road can be hard to resist.

above right: Traveling with the locals in India.

Some routes are considered difficult due to the condition of the roads or the standard of the local driving. There are countries that more naturally lend themselves to relaxed, leisurely riding, combining great roads with sightseeing, good food, and accommodation. And then there are routes that really are designed for full-throttle riding. There are also roads that will take you to some of the most beautiful scenery on earth. It is impossible to include all the great riding that some countries offer, but the routes featured provide a flavor of the type of riding you can expect. Many fantastic motorcycle destinations did not make it into the book, either because bike hire or bike-inclusive tours were not available, because the length of the journey was longer than an average vacation, or because current political situations advised avoidance. The Karakorum Highway in Pakistan is an incredible ride, yet a lack of reasonable bike hire and current travel restrictions meant it did not make the final selection. However, these limitations can, and hopefully will, change and open up even more destinations to intrepid motorcyclists.

Coming face-to-face with Africa's wildlife.

Researching this book has been immensely enjoyable, and it has brought back memories of the amazing trips I have taken and the good friends I have made. I have spoken to friends across the globe about their favorite roads and why that journey was so special. I have met operators who started their own tour company purely for the pleasure of meeting other riders and showing them the amazing riding possibilities in their country. The one thing that everyone has in common is their enthusiasm and passion for riding motorcycles.

The Bike

One of the advantages of hiring a bike on arrival is that you get to ride a completely different machine from the bike you have at home. I have occasionally mentioned a particular type of bike when it is so much a part of the experience of the journey. If you've always been a sports-bike rider, then perhaps hire a Harley in the USA, or, if you have always ridden dual sport bikes, opt for a classic Enfield Bullet in India. The bike you choose can enhance the experience, and may even convert you to a machine you would never otherwise ride. Some countries offer a wide choice of hire bikes, others perhaps only one or two models. Have you ever wondered what it would be like tackling dirt roads on a Belarusian Minsk 125cc? Try it – you may be pleasantly surprised.

If you choose to travel alone, you can be sure of meeting like-minded friends along the way.

If you plan on taking your own bike, it really isn't necessary to splurge on a new, fully kitted tourer. If you are comfortable with your current bike, then always consider taking it. A motorcycle will go anywhere; some are just better suited to challenging terrain than others. There is an amazing choice of great motorcycles, and the decision is generally down to your budget or favored brand. Look at your chosen route, comfort, and luggage-carrying capacity. The bike's off-road ability and fuel range may also have a bearing. There are no hard and fast rules. All types of motorcycle can be, and have been, used for journeys across the globe.

The world feels closer to you on a motorcycle than it does when you are enclosed in a car.

Travel Requirements

The internet has made planning a motorcycle trip so much easier. It is now possible to arrange bike hire, book organized trips, or arrange the freight of your own machine with the click of a computer mouse. You can read about other people's journeys and email questions to riders on the other side of the globe. This book does not go into any detail regarding visas, *carnets de passage* or health checks, as these all differ depending on nationality and can change regularly and without warning. Half the fun of any motorcycle trip is in the excitement of planning the route, deciding the type of riding you want to experience, and choosing the bike. Ultimately, everyone's trip is unique, and the final decision regarding route and motorcycle will be yours.

Final Words

As you load up your bike, the anticipation of the adventures in store, the challenge of the riding ahead, and the knowledge that you and your motorcycle can go anywhere is a feeling that only motorcyclists can describe. Setting out on any motorcycle journey is supremely exciting, and I hope that the following journeys will inspire you to break out and explore the world on, without doubt, the very best form of motorized transport: the motorcycle.

You won't just meet other people on the road—you might make some friends of other species, too.

AFRICA

Dune riding in spectacular scenery.

The Tizi n'Test Pass in the High Atlas Mountains.

MOROCCO

CEUTA TO MARRAKECH LOOP

**This route encompasses the Atlas Mountains,
the deserts of the Sahara, and the wild Atlantic coast.**

Mysterious Morocco is so close to Europe, yet seems a world and several centuries away. The colorful bazaars of the imperial cities, the deserts of the Sahara, and the lush palm-filled oases all provide a tantalizing taste of North Africa. There are accommodation options for every budget, from desert campsites to luxurious *riads* (traditional Moroccan dwellings with interior gardens). The sheer diversity of the landscape and culture is hard to beat, making a visit to Morocco a wonderfully varied and rewarding experience.

Morocco is a fantastic winter escape for motorcyclists, offering an exciting range of riding possibilities. Time and ability really aren't an issue since there is just so much choice, with plenty of well-maintained roads connecting the main sights. Two of the best road-riding routes in Morocco take you over the high passes of the Tizi n'Tichka and the Tizi n'Test and both connect the desert towns of the south to the imperial city of Marrakech. For off-road riders there are mule tracks, dry riverbeds, deep sand, and plenty of *fesh fesh* (bulldust, or sand as fine as talcum powder) to test your skills. Fuel is easily available throughout the country, but check in advance where your next fuel stop is located if you head off-road or into the desert.

The Route

Allow roughly two weeks for the following route, which combines great road riding with city sightseeing, desert and mountain scenery, and wild Atlantic beaches.

Roll off the ferry at Spanish-owned Ceuta, entering Morocco at the northern tip. Head south for 62 miles (100 km) through the wild and isolated Rif Mountains to Chefchaouen, a picturesque town of narrow streets and blue-washed houses nestled between two mountains. Enjoy the

A bustling souk in Marrakech, Morocco.

relaxed atmosphere for a few days, then head south to Fez. The little-used but absolutely awesome switchbacks of the Route de l'Unité, via Ketama, wind for over 168 miles (270 km) through the wild, lawless heart of the Rif region, where *kif* (marijuana) covers the surrounding hills and is the main economy of the region. The medina (literally "city," now used to refer to the original Arab part of any Moroccan town) in Fez is one of the largest in the world. Thousands of craftsmen work in a warren of souks, or bazaars, their tiny shops spilling out onto noisy, pungent alleyways that lead to palaces, mosques, and *medersas* (student residencies). Leave your bike (and those heavy boots!) at the hotel and lose yourself in Morocco's oldest imperial city.

Sahara-bound, the 270-mile (435-km) ride south to Erfoud crosses the Middle and High Atlas mountains. The traffic is light and road surfaces are generally good, making the ride enjoyable and reasonably fast. Once over the Atlas at Errachidia, the plains and palmeries start to melt into the Sahara proper.

From Erfoud, ride out to the Erg Chebbi sand dunes and perfect your sand-riding techniques, or exchange your motorcycle for a camel and head into the desert for a few days. Once you've finished playing in the sand, take the road west for about 78 miles (125 km), cutting through palmeries to the magnificent gorges of Todra and Boumalne Dades. Road bikes will have no problem negotiating the 16-mile (25-km) paved road at either entrance, and riders on a dual sport bike can follow the well-maintained tracks that connect the two. There are a number of small hotels within the gorges, so stay overnight and watch the setting sun turn the gorges crimson while sipping "whiskey berber."

From Boumalne Dades, head 84 miles (135 km) west to Ouarzazate, the largest town in the south and the start of a ride to Marrakech via the fabulous Tizi n'Tichka Pass (P31). The winding but well-paved 106-mile (170-km) road is lined with Berber villages and crumbling kasbahs, or citadels. It can easily be ridden in a day, but there are numerous opportunities to detour from the main road. About an hour north of Ouarzazate, a 12-mile (20-km) road runs off to the magnificent kasbah of Ait-Ben-Haddou. This is probably the most famous and best preserved of the Moroccan kasbahs, due to its appearance in a number of Hollywood films, such as *Lawrence of Arabia* and *Gladiator*. An overnight stop in the nearby village ensures fabulous views of the kasbah over breakfast.

Bike: It is possible to take your own bike into Morocco, but you will need a Green Card. Bike hire is available in Marrakech. There are operators in Marrakech, Ouarzazate, and Spain offering bike-inclusive tours.

Weather Watch: Morocco is a year-round destination. However, June to September is very hot, especially in the desert. Expect snow in the mountains from November to February.

Extending the Ride: A short ferry ride from Tangier or Ceuta will take you to Andalucía in southern Spain.

Boumalne Dades at dusk.

Rejoining the main road, watch out for the turnoff to a bumpy track about 31 miles (50 km) further north. The 27-mile (44-km) track takes you to the crumbling atmospheric kasbah of Telouet, set against a backdrop of stark mountains that turn almost black in the changing light. If you have a dual sport bike, there is a challenging track connecting these two kasbahs. For an insight into the dramatic history and intrigue of the rulers of the House of Glaoua, read Gavin Maxwell's excellent *Lords of the Atlas*.

Return to the main road for the final 68 miles (110 km) to Marrakech. Be warned, though, that negotiating the labyrinthine alleys of the old city can be hair-raising as you vie for space with donkeys, tradesmen, and stray dogs. Spend a few days soaking up the atmosphere of this medieval city that seems unchanged by the centuries, and watch in amusement as acrobats, storytellers, and snake charmers skillfully extract dirhams from visitors and locals alike on the Djemma el Fna. However, if you just cannot get enough of the twisting, mountainous roads, then load up the bike and head south once more to the fabulous Tizi n'Test Pass (S501). The road is remote and cuts through the heart of the Atlas, linking Marrakech with the Souss plain and the deserts beyond. Hairpin bends and spectacular views abound for more than 137 miles (220 km) to the busy trading town of Taroudant in the Souss Valley, which is hidden from view on the approach by its red mud walls.

From Taroudant, head west for an hour to the coast. The route north to Ceuta hugs the Atlantic, following well-maintained roads, including a section of motorway. There are numerous towns and villages along the coast and the pretty white-washed town of Essaouira, a 162-mile (260-km) ride north from Taroudant, is a relaxing place to spend a few days before continuing for a further 249 miles (400 km) up the coast to Rabat. A mix of French-styled boulevards and historical Arab monuments, Rabat feels surprisingly sleepy for a capital city. From here a 199-mile (320-km) ride north takes you to back to Ceuta, leaving a country that should have you already planning your next trip as the ferry heads back across the Strait of Gibraltar.

Morocco is an ideal winter escape.

The stunning Great Rift Valley in Africa

KENYA

NAIROBI TO THE CENTRAL HIGHLANDS AND THE GREAT RIFT VALLEY

From Nairobi, ride to the lush Central Highlands and the jagged, snow-capped peaks of Mount Kenya, crossing the equator on stunning roads that link the lakes and canyons of the Great Rift Valley.

The Central Highlands and Great Rift Valley provide an amazing variety of landscapes and wildlife. Tropical jungle and lush plantations give way to forested escarpments and spectacular valleys, revealing vast lakes teeming with birdlife. The beautiful acacia forests of Lake Nakuru National Park—made famous in the film *Out of Africa*—boast an incredible variety of wildlife. Kenya's impressive accommodations are all part of the experience and are a wonderful treat after a long day's ride. Kick off your boots and relax in style at luxurious lodges and tented camps that afford stunning views of waterholes or mountain peaks.

Good tarmac gives way to bumpy, potholed roads, then reappears again for long stretches. Unlike some parts of Africa, where roads quickly become impassable with a little rain, the main road surfaces of northern Kenya are generally good. This is a motorcycle ride in Africa that will take you to mountains, valleys, and game parks along roads that, while never perfect, do not require off-road skills, a fully loaded dual sport, or a week's supply of fuel. The riding is fun and not too hurried as you travel along roads dug from a rich, red volcanic earth that contrast beautifully with the surrounding lush, green vegetation.

The Route

This route takes you through the Central Highlands and across the Great Rift and should take a week to ten days, allowing time to combine your riding with game drives and highland walks.

Ride out of Nairobi heading for Mount Kenya about 152 miles (245 km) northeast. The area is extensively farmed, and Kenya's excellent coffee is cultivated in this rich, volcanic soil. As you ride, Mount Kenya is visible in the distance, its twin peaks often shrouded in cloud. It

above: Flamingos at Lake Bogoria, Kenya.

below: The official equator line in Nanyuki, Kenya.

is a stunningly beautiful mountain, and at 17,058 feet (5,199 m) is Africa's second-highest peak. The town of Naro Moru is about 109 miles (175 km) north of Nairobi on the A2. Stay in a lodge in the area for fabulous views of Mount Kenya, and hire guides for the trek to the peak or to take a wonderful day-walk up the lower slopes, passing through lush, tropical vegetation and amazing plants.

From Naro Moru, continue north for about an hour (A2) to the equator sign at Nanyuki, which is certainly worth a photograph from astride your motorcycle. Skirt the equator for about 62 miles (100 km) along a largely unsealed road (C76) to Nyahururu—Kenya's highest town at 7,743 feet (2,360 m)—then drop southwest (B5), descending into the Great Rift Valley, and arriving at Lake Nakuru National Park before sunset. In addition to its famous flamingo population, Nakuru is also a great place to see black and white rhinos, and leopard sightings are frequent. Park your bike for a couple of days and take advantage of the game drives offered by the lodges and campsites in and around the park. Temperatures rise dramatically and vegetation becomes sparser as you ride the 57 miles (85 km) north from Nakuru to Lake Bogoria, a soda lake of boiling-hot springs, geysers, and steam jets. Thousands of flamingos and birds inhabit a lake surrounded by a barren and rocky landscape, evidence of the volcanic origins of the Rift Valley. In stark contrast, the freshwater Lake Baringo, less than an hour's ride north, is a lush, green oasis. It lies at an altitude of 3,609 feet (1,100 m) and is surrounded by mountains rising to almost 9,843 feet (3,000 m). Unpack the panniers and spend a few days relaxing beside the lake and exploring the area on two wheels minus your luggage. Join an early morning boat trip to see fish eagles, crocodiles, and hippos, then take a fantastic 170-mile (273-km) loop over the Tugen Hills into the Kerio Valley. From the town of Marigat, central to both lakes, ride a paved road that climbs and winds through magnificent scenery across canyons and ridges to Kabarnet in the Tugen Hills, then plunge from the Elgeyo Escarpment into the beautiful Kerio Valley. Visit the small town of Iten, "Home of Champions," famous for being the center of Kenyan middle- and long-distance running, before returning to your base on beautiful Lake Baringo for a nice evening while watching the hippos leave the water to graze.

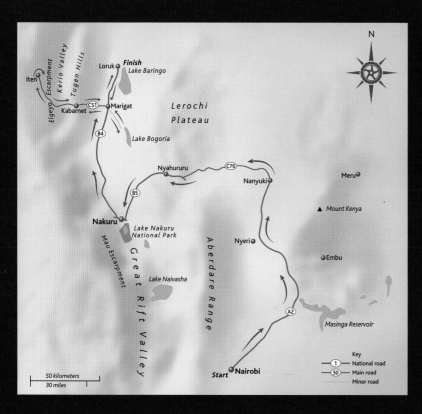

Bike: It is possible to take your own bike into Kenya. A *Carnet de Passage en Douane* (CPD) is usually required in Africa. Bike hire is available in Nairobi. There are operators based in Nairobi and Mombasa offering bike-inclusive tours.

Weather Watch: December to mid-March is the best time to visit, although there can be light rains in December. The wettest period is April and May.

Extending the Ride: No overland connection to other featured journeys.

African sunset.

Expect to see stunning desert scenery in Namibia.

NAMIBIA

WINDHOEK TO ETOSHA NATIONAL PARK

This route ventures south from Windhoek to the sand dunes of the Namib Desert before heading north through the remote, arid wilderness and desolate mountain scenery of Damaraland to Etosha National Park.

Namibia is a country of contrasts and one of Africa's best-kept secrets. Ride past table-topped mountains, through lunar landscapes, and across vast open plains, enjoying an exhilarating sense of space and freedom. Discover the colossal sand dunes of the world's oldest desert and exquisite rock art that has survived for thousands of years in cool canyons, away from the scorching heat. Meet the beautiful tribal people who populate this ancient land and experience the unforgettable sight of rare desert elephants and black rhino crossing the road ahead of you as they roam freely.

A network of well-maintained, graded gravel roads crisscross the country—about 70 percent of Namibia's roads are unsealed. In the dry season it is not difficult to ride on the loose mix of sand and gravel, and the roads are well signposted, but avoid the rainy season when rivers can flood the roads. Negotiate dry riverbeds, cross patches of sand, and ride all day on empty roads that stretch as far as the eye can see. The heat haze sits on the horizon as you weave through vast expanses of arid wilderness, leaving a trail of dust in your wake. There are luxurious lodges and tented camps, but pack your tent well—this is a motorcycle journey that lends itself to days of solitary riding and nights spent under thousands of stars beside a glowing campfire.

The Route

A week to ten days will give you time to combine riding with a visit to some of Namibia's top sights.

Head straight for the Namib Desert about 250 miles (400 km) southwest (C26/C14) of Windhoek. The gravel road takes you through the Khomas Hochland Mountains, climbs the Kupferberg Pass, passes by fantastic views from the Spreetshoogte Pass, and descends into the Namib Desert at Sesriem, gateway to the world's highest dunes. Stay in a luxury lodge or camp

under the shade of acacia trees and gaze at the night stars, rising early to watch the sunrise over the dunes.

Enjoy the cool desert air as you ride into the Tsauchab Valley on a road that is paved for 27 miles (60 km), followed by 3 miles (5 km) through heavy sand to the dunes at Sossusvlei. There is a shuttle service if you don't want to ride this final tricky section. The mountainous dunes are an awesome 985 feet (300 m) high and dwarf everything in sight. Sculpted by the wind, the shifting sands are constantly changing shape, while the movement of the hot desert sun changes the dunes' color throughout the day, culminating in a fiery display at sunset.

From Sesriem, head north on gravel roads for about 186 miles (300 km) (C19/C14) via the Gaub Pass and the spectacular barren landscape of Kuiseb Canyon. Join a paved road for the short final section from the port town of Walvis Bay to Swakopmund, a charming coastal town and a center for activity-based sports. The nearby dunes provide the opportunity to spend a day quad-biking or dune-boarding.

From Swakopmund, the road follows the coast north for about 47 miles (75 km) to Henties Bay, where you head inland (C35) riding deep into the dry desert landscape of Damaraland along long stretches of road and across dry riverbeds. In the Twyfelfontein area, follow dusty tracks to ancient bushman rock art and a petrified forest that is more than 200 million years old. End your long (217-mile/350-km) day's ride below Brandberg Mountain as it glows in the setting sun before making camp nearby on the banks of the Aba-Huab River and enjoying a campfire supper under wide African skies.

The mountain scenery in Namibia makes for an unforgettable trip.

Bike: It is possible to take your own bike into Namibia. Bike hire is available in Windhoek. There are operators offering bike-inclusive tours.

Weather Watch: May to October is the best time to visit. November to March is the wettest period.

Extending the Ride: Link up to a trip in neighboring South Africa. It is about 932 miles (1,500 km) from Windhoek to Cape Town, or a two-hour flight.

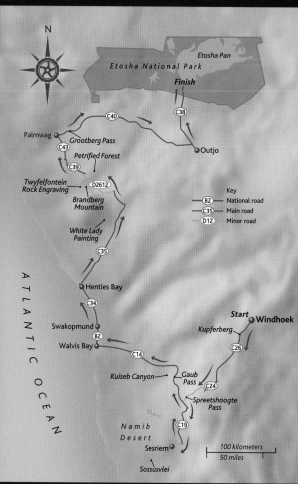

Rising early next morning, ride into the vast plains of northern Damaraland, scouring the landscape as you ride in search of the elusive desert elephants. Comfortable tented camps scatter this remote region, many offering guided wildlife tours, so slow the pace and take time to enjoy this rugged landscape.

Refuel at Palmwag before the ride up and over the Grootberg Pass, heading east for about 155 miles (250 km) to join the C38, which leads to the main entrance of Etosha National Park. Wash off the dust and relax at comfortable lodges, and don't neglect to take a guided drive into the park to observe the rare and endangered wildlife that roam one of the greatest game parks in southern Africa.

Cape Point, where the Atlantic and Indian Oceans meet.

SOUTH AFRICA

CAPE TOWN CIRCUIT THROUGH THE GARDEN ROUTE

Ride a circular route of the Western and Eastern capes that encompass South Africa's coast, plains, and winelands.

Beautiful, cosmopolitan Cape Town nestles in the shadow of Table Mountain; it's an inviting and relaxed city and the perfect starting point for a ride through the Western Cape and Eastern Cape. Roads weave through the tranquil valleys of the winelands, follow the coastal Garden Route past forested mountains and white-sand beaches, and then head inland to the endless skies and vast plains of the Karoo. The region offers accommodation to suit all tastes and budgets, an incredible variety of seafood, and, of course, South Africa's award-winning wines.

South Africa has long been a favorite motorcycle destination. Its wide choice of bike hire and fabulous roads make it an easy and enjoyable fly-ride trip. The Western and Eastern capes have great tarmac roads that wind through stunning scenery and a Mediterranean climate that all motorcyclists love. There are also plenty of opportunities to get off-road and put that hired dual sport bike to the test.

The Route

Allowing for sightseeing and time off the bike, this is roughly a two-week circuit that sticks to the tarmac but with options to get on the dirt.

Leaving Cape Town, the fun begins just east of Hout Bay along Chapman's Peak Drive, 6 miles (10 km) of thrilling, twisting riding along a cliff edge road that boasts an incredible 114 curves, the wild Atlantic Ocean swirling below. The road leads to the Cape of Good Hope, where the Atlantic and Indian oceans smash into each other at Cape Point. Dismount for a few moments to absorb the fantastic views of the crashing surf and the dramatic windswept coastline.

Leave the Cape via False Bay, following the coast road (R44) from the Strand to Hermanus, which lies about 71 miles (115 km) east of Cape Town and is famed for its seafood and visiting whales. An enjoyable 93 miles (150 km) of sweeping bends lead slightly inland (R326) before dropping south to Cape L'Agulhas, the southernmost point of Africa. Spend the night here or further down the coast at the pretty village of Arniston.

A 155-mile (250-km) ride northeast on the N2 takes you to Mossel Bay, the start of the famous Garden Route, which runs for 115 miles (185 km) to Storms River Mouth. The road winds through tranquil countryside, below rocky cliffs, and alongside wild, sandy beaches. It can easily be ridden in a few hours, but with a wide choice of hotels and restaurants scattered along the route, it is worth a few days' leisurely ride. Adrenaline junkies can rappel, bungee jump, and even swim with sharks. About halfway along, the pretty town of Knysna makes

Riding the sand dunes in South Africa.

a good overnight stop. The town is surrounded by a beautiful lagoon that empties into the Indian Ocean at the dramatic cliffs known as the Heads. Overnight here and dine on the towns' specialty: delicious, fresh oysters.

Heading into the Eastern Cape, leave the N2 briefly and detour onto the old road (R102) for a scenic, twisting ride over the Grootrivier and Bloukrans passes, then drop down to Storms River Mouth and Tsitsikamma National Park, an area of rocky coast and indigenous ancient forest, with a marine reserve that stretches more than 3 miles (5 km) out to sea. Port Elizabeth, a further 124 miles (200 km) east (N2), is where you leave the coast behind and head inland for about 186 miles (300 km) toward the Karoo Nature Reserve and the semi-desert of the African bush. There are a number of game reserves within an easy ride of Port Elizabeth, all offering accommodation and wildlife safaris. A ride north (N10) over the Olifantskop Pass leads you to the turnoff for Addo Elephant National Park and the chance to see big game.

Returning to the main road (N10), pick up the R63 at Cookhouse for a 93-mile (150-km) ride to the historic town of Graaff-Reinet in the heartland of the Great Karoo. Just out of town, ride along a narrow, paved road that climbs the mountains for stunning sunset views down to the Valley of Desolation. Stay in the area and experience life on a sheep farm at one of the traditional farmsteads.

If you are lucky, encounters with wildlife will be part of your African adventure.

Bike: It is possible to take your own bike into South Africa. Bike hire is available in Cape Town. There are operators offering bike-inclusive tours.

Weather Watch: South Africa is a year-round destination. Summer on the Cape is between November and February or March.

Extending the Ride: Link up to a trip in neighboring Namibia. It is about 932 miles (1,500 km) from Cape Town to Windhoek, or a two-hour flight.

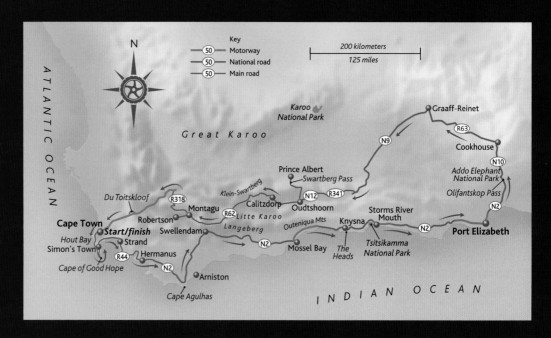

Vast horizons surround you on the fast 186-mile (300-km) ride (N9) through flat plains to Oudtshoorn, the principle town of Little Karoo. Base yourself in the area for a few days and take advantage of the great riding on offer. Oudtshoorn grew rich from the Victorian fashion featuring large feathers; for the lighter-framed motorcyclist, there is even the chance to visit a farm and take an ostrich ride. If that doesn't get the adrenaline going, then take a ride in to "Hell." Gamkaskloof, commonly known as Die Hel or "The Hell," is an awesome dirt road that leads to a dramatic valley forming part of the Swartberg Nature Reserve. It is reached from the summit of the Swartberg Pass (R328), which lies between Oudtshoorn and the town of Prince Albert, 43 miles (70 km) north. If you want to spend the night in Die Hel, there are camping facilities in the valley. Alternatively, take a ride over the unpaved mountain hairpins of the Swartberg Pass, returning to Oudtshoorn via the

paved Meiringspoort Pass, which crosses the Groot River 26 times. The mountains and valleys of Little Karoo are connected by a series of fantastic passes that twist, climb, and switchback through a wild, rugged landscape.

Leave Oudtshoorn, heading west on Route 62. A 137-mile (220-km) ride brings you to the town of Robertson, one of the main lovely towns of the winelands, which lie just a few hours east of Cape Town. Stay at one of the traditional farmsteads near Franschhoek or Stellenbosch, enjoy local food and wine, and take a ride out to the historic estates and vineyards that nestle below towering mountains.

Riding through "Hell."

THE AMERICAS

Monument Valley, Navajo Tribal Park.

A glacier in the Columbia Icefields in the Rockies.

CANADA

THE ROCKIES: CALGARY TO JASPER

This route runs from Calgary to Jasper National Park, through the heart of the Canadian Rockies.

The Canadian Rockies run through the provinces of Alberta and British Columbia in western Canada, spanning almost 932 miles (1,500 km) as far as the Yukon border. Soaring peaks tower over a pristine, unspoiled wilderness of forest, glacial lakes, canyons, and valleys. The sheer immensity and beauty of the landscape is hard to imagine and the scenery that unfolds before you will surpass all expectations.

There is a short summer season for a motorcycle trip in the Rockies, when the snow has finally melted and it is warm enough to hit the road on a bike. This is a ride through Canada's big outdoors; the weather can quickly change, so pack plenty of layers. The main road surfaces are excellent, giving you time to admire breathtaking views from the saddle. Snow-capped peaks appear around every bend and there are regular viewpoints along the way for you to pull over and admire the scenery. The ride along the Icefields Parkway is absolutely spectacular and has to rate as one of the world's classic motorcycle rides.

The Route

A week will allow for time exploring the national parks while riding this 280-mile (450-km) route.

The city of Calgary nestles between the Rockies and the rolling prairies and provides the perfect springboard for a ride into the Rockies themselves. It is a fast and pleasant 81-mile (130-km) ride on the Trans-Canada Highway to

Banff National Park. The resort town of Banff is lively and the main base for exploring the wooded valleys, peaks, and crystal waters of possibly the most famous park of the Canadian Rockies.

From Banff, take the scenic Bow Valley Parkway to Lake Louise. It is a short ride at just over 34 miles (55 km), but the views are magnificent, so slow down the pace, relax into the ride, and enjoy the scenery. The village of Lake Louise is located in the Bow Valley and provides accommodation and information. The lake itself lies just 3 miles (4 km) above the village along the winding Lake Louise Drive. Turquoise blue and dominated by the Victoria Glacier, it is a truly breathtaking sight, its perfection seeming almost unreal. An enjoyable, winding 8-mile (13-km) ride leads to the smaller—but possibly even more beautiful—Moraine Lake, its waters surrounded by ten glaciated summits.

Returning to Lake Louise, head north to Jasper National Park along the snow-capped Icefields Parkway, which cuts through the heart of the Rockies and crosses through both Banff and Jasper National Parks. Ride the 143 miles (230 km) in a day or pull over for a few nights on the way and explore the region. There are campsites, youth hostels, and a few hotels along the route. Described by early fur traders as the "Wonder Trail," the unending succession of gorgeous turquoise lakes, vast walls of ice, and row after row

above: The Icefields Parkway cuts through the Rockies and offers spectacular views.

below: The stunning views at Peyto Lake should not be missed.

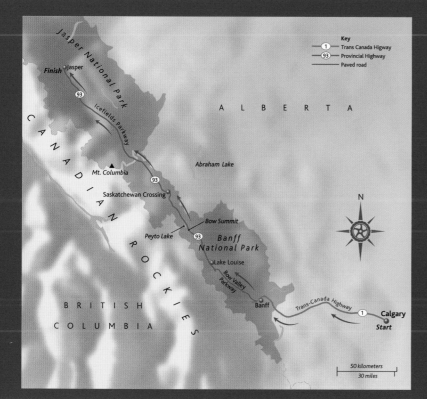

Bike: It is possible to take your own bike into Canada. Bike hire is available in Calgary or Vancouver. There are operators offering bike-inclusive tours.

Weather Watch: June to September is really the only time to ride this route by motorcycle.

Extending the Ride: Link this trip with a ride in the Yukon and Northwest Territories. Anchorage is 2,130 miles (3,438 km) from Calgary and Whitehorse is 1,425 miles (2,293 km).

of jagged peaks provides unforgettable views for most of the ride. The road climbs steadily for 25 miles (40 km) through a sub-alpine forest up to Bow Summit, which, at 6,785 feet (2,068m), is the highest point on the parkway. The fantastic views at the nearby Peyto Lake viewpoint should not be missed.

The road then starts to drop for the following 23 miles (37 km) to Saskatchewan Crossing, where you can fill your tank with gas before the steep climb toward the Columbia Icefields, the largest collection of ice and snow in the Rockies. You can take a Snocoach tour or even an ice-walk right out onto the Athabasca Glacier. From here, the road begins a gradual descent toward the sleepy town of Jasper at the end of the parkway. Roll into town and enjoy its laid-back atmosphere while you explore the huge, rugged wilderness of Jasper National Park.

Riding in the Rockies.

The busy skyline of Québec City.

CANADA

MONTRÉAL TO THE GASPÉ PENINSULA

Ride from Montréal following the north shore of the Saint Lawrence River to Baie-Comeau, crossing to the scenic roads of the Gaspé Peninsula.

French-speaking Québec is totally unique within North America. A province of contrasts, it blends old world and new, featuring stylish cities within an awe-inspiring wilderness. Stretching almost 1,243 miles (2,000 km) from north to south, the northern regions encompass enormous expanses of forest and tundra. Southern Québec is easily accessible and split by the St. Lawrence River, which flows from the Great Lakes to the Atlantic Ocean.

On this route, you can dine on fine French cuisine and ride the Chemin du Roy ("Royal Way"). Follow the Saint Lawrence River on winding roads and through pretty villages along La Route des Baleines ("The Whale Route"), then cross to the Gaspé Peninsula, which juts more than 310 miles (500 km) into the ocean. This is a motorcycle ride that takes you through a land of mountains, vast lakes, and mighty rivers. With a good range of accommodation options and the choice of riding short daily distances, it is a journey that can be done at a leisurely pace.

The Route

The following route gives you a taste of the southeast region of this huge country. Ten days to two weeks will allow for time off the bike to explore the national parks.

From Montréal, motor along the Chemin du Roy. This route was built in 1735 to link Montréal, Trois-Rivières, and Québec City, and for over a

The leisurely pace of this journey is well suited to its gentle landscape.

Parked to take a break in Montréal.

century conveyed mail and travelers by stagecoach or sleigh via 29 relay stations. At full gallop, the journey could be made in two days. Today it is an easy day's ride, as HW138 follows the old road for approximately 155 miles (250 km). You will ride through beautiful scenery and picturesque villages along the north shore of the mighty Saint Lawrence River toward Québec City, a capital that combines its modern French style with ancient cobbled streets and historic buildings.

From Québec City, take La Route des Baleines, which runs for 165 miles (266 km) to Baie-Comeau, where you cross to the Gaspé Peninsula. Running through the beautiful UNESCO-protected Charlevoix region, which stretches from the Beaupré Coast to the Saguenay Fjord, the road (HW138) winds through rural villages, valleys, and rolling hills.

At the pretty town of Baie-Saint-Paul, take the coast-hugging HW362, which twists and turns through many hilltop villages. The soft landscape eventually gives way to more dramatic rocky outcrops and sheer cliffs, where the Saguenay River meets one of the world's longest fjords and smashes its way into the St. Lawrence River. This mixing of the cold seawaters with the freshwater of the Saguenay River produces a rich crop of plankton, and in the summer months, migratory whales flock to the area to feed. To see so many species of whale in one area is a magical and humbling experience.

Bike: It is possible to take your own bike into Canada. Bike hire is available in Montréal. There are operators offering bike-inclusive tours.

Weather Watch: Mid-May to mid-October is the best time to visit.

Extending the Ride: Head from Montréal to Vermont for a ride around New England, or, from the Gaspé Peninsula, ride through New Brunswick to Nova Scotia and onto Newfoundland.

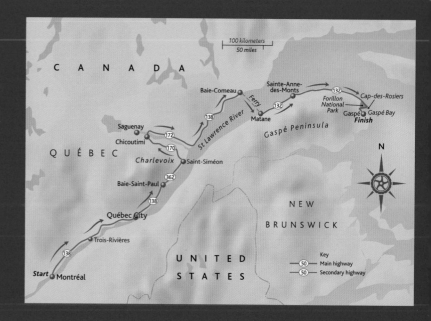

From Saint-Siméon, the HW170 twists its way for 78 miles (125 km) to the Saguenay Fjord National Park, hitting the enormous fjord after about 31 miles (50 km). There are no bridges until the crossing at Chicoutimi, where you can return along the opposite side of the fjord (HW172), picking up the main highway (HW132). Again, follow the HW132 for another 125 miles (200 km) to Baie-Comeau, passing lakes, forests, and sandy inlets. A ferry crosses to Matane on the northern shores of the mountainous Gaspé Peninsula, where ravines cut through forested slopes and mountains tumble to a ragged coastline. This is superb motorcycle country, with enough riding and walking routes to occupy you for days. The road (HW132) hugs the coastline around the peninsula, sometimes squeezing between the ocean and the mountains. It twists and turns, passing picturesque coves and coastal villages, through the Forillon National Park and on to Gaspé Bay for fantastic ocean views where, in 1534, French explorer Jacques Cartier "discovered" the Gulf of St. Lawrence, which he named Canada.

The dramatic scenery of the Gaspé Peninsula.

Gros Morne National Park, Newfoundland.

CANADA

THE GULF OF MAINE TO THE STRAIT OF BELLE ISLE

Follow the lovely Nova Scotia coast and journey to the remote Great Northern Peninsula of Newfoundland.

The North Atlantic will be your constant companion as you tour wild and remote Nova Scotia and Newfoundland. Cruise the Lighthouse Route through picturesque fishing villages and historic seafaring towns, and ride the twisting, mountainous roads of the Cabot Trail for far-reaching ocean views. Discover the isolation and splendid natural beauty of Newfoundland as you ride alongside whales, seabirds, and icebergs.

With over 4,350 miles (7,000 km) of winding coastal roads, there are plenty of opportunities to pull over and relax on a ride through Nova Scotia. The pace cranks up a notch in Newfoundland, as distances between towns are long and the weather is unpredictable. In both Nova Scotia and Newfoundland, the North Atlantic weather takes its toll on the roads; do not expect perfect tarmac, and make sure you pack your waterproofs. This route offers great riding, quiet roads, and stunning natural beauty.

The Route

The following route gives you a flavor of Nova Scotia and a taste of the vast island of Newfoundland. Two weeks will allow for time off the bike to explore the national parks.

The seaside town of Yarmouth is the starting point for the scenic Lighthouse Route, which follows the southern shore, hugging the coast for just

above: HOG (Harley Owners'
Group) rally in Cape Breton.

below: Cruising the Cabot Trail
on Cape Breton Island.

under 373 miles (600 km). The riding is leisurely as you cruise into the historic port towns and fishing villages that line the route. The waters teem with marine life, ensuring fresh seafood is brought in daily. What better way to end your day's ride than feasting upon lobster, tuna, or mussels washed down with wines from the Annapolis Valley? The Lighthouse Route ends at the vibrant capital of Halifax.

Continue following the coast east of Halifax along HW7, which cuts inland after about 109 miles (175 km) heading north, then east to the Strait of Canso and the narrow causeway that links the rest of Nova Scotia to Cape Breton Island. The Cabot Trail is a stunningly scenic loop of 185 miles (300 km), encompassing woodland, soaring mountains, rocky cliffs, and beaches as it skirts the edge of Cape Breton Highlands National Park. The highway is carved into the side of mountains; wide, sweeping bends rise and dip, affording amazing views of the Atlantic Ocean and the Gulf of St. Lawrence.

Leaving the Cabot Trail, an hour's ride takes you to North Sydney for the 14-hour ferry trip to Newfoundland. The locals simply call it "The Rock." You land in Argentia on the southwest corner of the Avalon Peninsula and take the beautiful 249-mile (400-km) loop that skirts the coast around the Avalon Wilderness Reserve. The rich waters of Bay Bulls and Witless Bay teem with

Bike: It is possible to take your own bike into Canada. Bike hire is available in Halifax and Hubbards, Nova Scotia. Harold and Wendy Nesbitt produce an excellent guide to motorcycling in Nova Scotia: *www.motorcycletourguidens.com/about-nova-scotia.*

Weather Watch: Weather is unpredictable even in the summer months. It can be warm and sunny as well as cool, wet, windy, and foggy. It's likely to be a little of everything.

Extending the Ride: Get the ferry from Yarmouth to Portland, Maine for a ride around New England, or ride through New Brunswick to the Gaspé Peninsula in Québec.

humpback and minke whales and millions of seabirds; occasionally icebergs drift into view. Next, head toward the capital St. John's and nearby Cape Spear, the easternmost place on the North American continent. From St. John's, get on HW1, the Trans-Canada Highway; it's the only main road running across the island's northern shore. The road cuts across the Terra Nova National Park and through the towns of Gander and Grand Falls for almost 373 miles (600 km) to Deer Lake, where you turn off onto Route 430 and the Viking Trail, which runs north for 304 miles (489 km). Enjoy the ride as fast, sweeping roads take you through Gros Morne National Park, a UNESCO World Heritage Site. The road leads to the moonscape of the Tablelands, a stunning glacier-carved fjord, and down to the water's edge at Rocky Harbor. The Viking Trail continues north to the Strait of Belle Isle and the remains of an 11th-century Norse colony at L'Anse aux Meadows, on the tip of the northern peninsula. As you stand next to your motorcycle looking out to sea, it isn't hard to imagine those Viking longships riding the winds on this wild, rugged coastline.

above: Baddeck Bay on Cape Breton Island, Nova Scotia.

The tranquil scenery of the Denali National Park, Alaska.

USA/CANADA

ALASKA: ANCHORAGE TO WHITEHORSE LOOP

Ride a great figure-eight loop through the wilds of the northeastern part of the North American continent.

It can be difficult to comprehend the sheer size and sparseness of population when first looking at a map of this area. Huge mountain ranges and snow-capped peaks are often visible as you ride along highways stretching off into the distance. The Yukon Territory is a vast area of forests, lakes, rivers, and rolling hills. The Saint Elias Mountains run through the southwest corner and contain Canada's highest peak, Mount Logan. In the west lie the famous Yukon and Klondike rivers, scene of North America's last great gold rush. Alaska consists of a giant plateau containing many long mountain ranges, which you will often ride alongside. In the center is Denali National Park. There are only two settlements of any size, Anchorage and Fairbanks; everything else is small by comparison, although good camping places and inexpensive hostels can be found along the route.

The area is not always in the grip of a deep freeze, and the riding conditions in summer can be excellent—but don't forget your waterproof gear, as rain is not uncommon. Mosquito repellent is also a must. Wildlife is abundant up here, and it is quite possible to see moose and bears by the road—just don't let them get too close! The road surfaces on this route are mostly excellent and nearly all sealed. You can hit the dirt on side trips if you wish, but a road bike will be perfectly adequate. Because of the mountainous terrain, there are plenty of twisting parts interspersed with long, fast straights, so lengthy distances can be covered quickly.

right: Dawson City was at the heart of the gold rush in the early 20th century.

below: Be sure to pack your cold weather gear when riding in Alaska.

The Route

This route will give a great taste of the semi-tamed wilderness in this part of the world. It can be ridden in two to three weeks with stops at places of interest, or even a short walk in one of the national parks if you would like a break from sitting on a bike.

The start of the trip is Alaska's capital, Anchorage. Head north on the state's only multi-lane highway, which you soon leave behind to join the George Parks Highway with the spectacular Chugach Mountains to your right. After 100 miles (161 km) of riding, reach the exit to the town of Talkeetna. This is the base for flights over the Denali Range, and it is well worth breaking your journey to take a flight over the giant glaciers and peaks. Denali National Park is to your left as you continue north over the 2,300-foot (701-m)-high Broad Pass to the park exit. Access is by shuttle bus only, but it is well worth a visit if you have the time. It is 360 miles (579 km) from Anchorage to Fairbanks, and the last section winds through the Tanana Hills, offering great riding with good views of the Alaska Range to the east. It is also one of the few places in Alaska where you can legally ride at 65 mph (105 kph)!

Fairbanks is only a quarter of the size of Anchorage and certainly feels like a town on the edge of things. It can reach -60°F (-51°C) in winter and 100°F (38°C) in summer—one of the biggest city temperature ranges in the world. Relax after a few long days in the saddle in one of the hot springs around town. It is here that you can turn north for a 900-mile (1,448-km) side trip up the Dalton Highway or Haul Road, crossing the Arctic Circle, and ending in Deadhorse. The road is unsealed and follows the Alaskan oil pipeline, crossing some of the most spectacular and wild terrain accessible in the state.

Leave Fairbanks and head southeast on the Alaska Highway through the great interior plateau. It is 200 miles (322 km) to Tok with only the small town of Delta Junction in between, so it can seem pretty lonely out there. Shortly after you reach Tetlin Junction, head off left onto what is called the Klondike Loop. This consists of the Taylor Highway (Alaska), Klondike (Canada), and the Top of the World Highway (Canada), and ends in Whitehorse in the Yukon Territory. The 280-mile (1,448-km) trip takes you through the town of Chicken, into the Yukon, and on to Dawson City. The Top of the World Highway is 200 miles (322 km) of wide, smooth dirt climbing over the alpine tundra, with fantastic views of the road running along ridgetops into the

Bike: It is possible to take your own bike into Canada and Alaska. You can hire bikes in Anchorage. There are operators offering bike-inclusive tours.

Weather Watch: Mid-May to mid-September is really the only time to ride this route by motorcycle.

Extending the Ride: Link this trip with a ride in the Canadian Rockies. Calgary is 2,130 miles (3,438 km) from Anchorage and 1,425 miles (2,293 km) from Whitehorse.

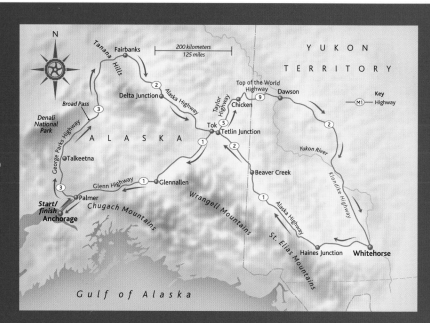

distance before you take the ferry over the Yukon River into town. Dawson City is a fascinating place and one of the highlights of the trip. It was once the center of the Klondike Gold Rush, and many old buildings have been restored. You can pan for gold and visit the largest wooden-hulled gold dredge in North America, which was built in 1912. From here it is 311 miles (500 km) to Whitehorse on the banks of the Yukon River, the largest city in northern Canada. Whitehorse also has its share of gold rush history, with a large restored paddle steamer berthed at the end of town.

Leaving Whitehorse, head 500 miles (805 km) northwest back on the Alaska Highway. After riding through the small settlement of Haines Junction, the Kluane Icefield Ranges and Saint Elias Mountains dominate the view to your left as you cruise along the perfect, sealed highway. Shortly after the town of Beaver Creek, cross back over the border into Alaska, headed back to Tok. From here it's time to complete the large figure-eight loop back to Anchorage along the Glenn Highway—a distance of 330 miles (531 km). Turn southwest and head to Glennallen along a beautiful stretch of road with the Wrangell Mountains to your left.

From Glennallen, the highway winds over the 3,000-foot (914-m) Tahneta Pass. This section is wonderfully scenic, especially in August when many trees turn gold and have a backdrop of snowy peaks and glaciers. You are on the last leg of your journey now through the town of Palmer to join the highway back into Anchorage, concluding your epic ride through the wilderness.

The St. Elias Mountains make a stunning backdrop.

Motoring along the roads of New England.

USA

BOSTON TO THE GREEN MOUNTAINS

From Boston, ride north along the Gulf of Maine, then head inland to the White Mountains of New Hampshire and the Green Mountains of Vermont.

If you enjoy riding on crisp autumn mornings when that chill in the air seems to make your bike run so much more smoothly and a late sunrise slowly illuminates the changing color of the trees, then head to New England for what has to be one of the world's finest natural displays. The forests of Maine, Vermont, and New Hampshire put on a flamboyant autumn show of fiery red maples, brilliant yellow birches, aspen, and poplars. The spectrum of color is intense and highlighted beautifully by the changing autumn skies.

An extravaganza of changing color combined with twisting mountain roads, rolling hills, and a relaxed pace of life has to be the ultimate autumn ride. These rural states just lend themselves to laid-back and lazy riding, and accommodation options are plentiful. A fun way to catch the headline acts in this spectacular show is to follow the daily bulletins and leave the planning of your route to Mother Nature, but if you prefer to combine catching the colors with some of New England's finest motorcycle roads, then some pre-planning ensures an amazing ride.

The Route

Spend a week following a route that combines coastal riding in Maine with rural roads that sweep through mountainous forests.

North of Boston, HW1 runs within a few miles of the coast, crossing the border into Maine just beyond Portsmouth. Ride alongside the wild and windswept coastline with the salt air on your face. With numerous scenic roads leading from HW1 to craggy coves, picturesque villages, and historic towns, this is a laid-back coastal ride offering time to partake in the local seafood, particularly lobsters.

above left: Forests of gold are a common sight.

above right: A river in the White Mountains.

Beautiful rural Vermont, where this journey finishes.

It is a beautiful 110-mile (177-km) ride from Boston to Portland, about halfway up the coast. En route, take a detour to the town of Salem, infamous for the Salem Witch Trails of 1692. A little further north, pull into the lovely coastal town of Kennebunkport. Portland itself is a small, beautiful city with a historic center, plenty of restaurants and cafés, and a lively waterfront. From Portland, head inland to Conway in New Hampshire, a ride of about 62 miles (100 km) (HW302). Spend days meandering along the lazy, winding roads within the White Mountain National Forest, where swathes of color surround you at every turn. Once an area of wilderness, the forests of the White Mountains are one of the star turns of the annual display. As foliage rides go, the twisting Kancamagus Highway (Route 112) running between Conway and Lincoln is unbeatable. "The Kank" is 34 miles (55 km) of sweeping views and spectacular sights, rising to almost 3,000 feet (914 m). At the height of autumn, traffic can be slow, but the beauty of traveling by bike is the fun of leaving the queues behind. Within the park, the Mount Washington Auto Road is an 8-mile (13-km) climb of endless hairpins and breathtaking views up the east side of the mountain. Check your brakes before attempting the journey down!

Weave your way southwest to Lebanon near the Connecticut River, the natural border with Vermont. It is a superb 51-mile (82-km) ride along Route

4 from Lebanon to Rutland and the Green Mountain National Forest. Rural Vermont is covered by mountainous forests that exhibit a mesmerizing spectrum of color. Its roads lead to sleepy hamlets of white, steepled churches and traditional country stores serving Vermont's specialty, maple syrup. Pull over for pancakes lavishly loaded with the sweetest syrup you have ever tasted, sure to keep your own engine running sweetly for hours.

New England is famous for its dazzling displays of autumnal color.

Bike: It is possible to take your own bike into the U.S. Bike hire is available in Boston, Portsmouth, and other major U.S. cities. There are operators offering year-round bike-inclusive tours.

Weather Watch: In the far north, fall starts in September; moving south, it runs to the end of October. Track the forecasts on one of the many websites devote to the season, such as *www.foliagenetwork.com.*

Extending the Ride: Ride from Vermont to Montréal in Québec, or take a boat from Portland, Maine to Yarmouth in Nova Scotia.

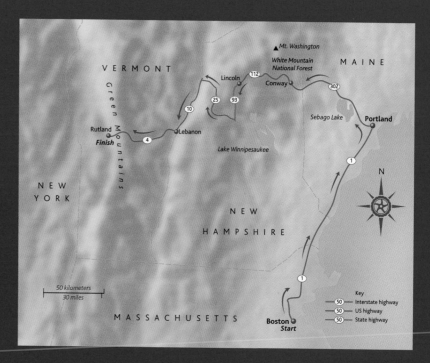

The Black Hills of South Dakota.

USA

DENVER TO DURANGO VIA THE BLACK HILLS OF SOUTH DAKOTA

Ride through Wyoming's wide-open prairies, through the Black Hills of South Dakota, and over mountain passes south to the lively town of Durango, Colorado.

Colorado is the state of continuous curves, crystal clear lakes, cliffs, and canyons. Clear mountain air, the smell of alpine forests, and abundant wildlife make for an exhilarating ride. Contrast Colorado's mountain scenery with the emptiness of Wyoming's windswept prairies and the Black Hills of South Dakota, home to many Native Americans.

Enjoy blue skies, bright sunshine, and magnificent mountain peaks as far as the eye can see as you negotiate hairpin bends on 12,000-foot (3,650-m) passes and ride the Trail Ridge Road—the highest continuous paved road in the United States. Rumble over Red Mountain Pass on the "Million Dollar Highway" and, if you time it right, you can party with 100,000 other motorcyclists at Sturgis, the world's largest motorcycle rally.

The Route

If you only have a week, start in Denver, then ride into the Rocky Mountains National Park and head south to Durango. If you can spare two weeks, head first into Wyoming and loop around the Black Hills before dropping back down to Colorado.

A 200-mile (322-km) ride north out of Denver across the plains of Wyoming brings you to Cheyenne and the world's largest outdoor rodeo. Consider staying the night and swapping your helmet for a Stetson, your Sidis for a pair of cowboy boots, and, if you are feeling really brave, a 70 bhp for one very raw bhp!

Leave town on HW85, following in the footsteps of the early pioneers as you ride across Wyoming's windswept, wide-open prairies, enjoying the sense of space as you edge open the throttle and ride into ancient Indian hunting grounds. Get onto the Iron Mountain Road

(HW16A), which spirals up the Black Hills of South Dakota. The road will take you on a scenic ride through Custer State Park, bringing you face-to-face with more than 1,500 bison. Be prepared to stop if they decide to cross the road! The road then leads via scenic tunnels to Mount Rushmore, where you can gaze upon the graven faces of four U.S. presidents.

Head to nearby Deadwood, a frontier town with a wild past. Characters such as Wild Bill Hickock, Calamity Jane, Wyatt Earp, and Doc Holliday graced its saloons and established its infamous reputation. These days the town offers a wide range of accommodation and makes a good base to explore the area. The town of Sturgis is just a short ride from Deadwood. If you are in the area in August, you must experience the Sturgis Rally. Started by the Jackpine Gypsies Motorcycle Club in 1938 with just nine racers, it is now one

Join the party at the Sturgis Rally.

of the oldest and largest motorcycle events, attracting riders from all over the world. Enjoy a week of music, motorcycles, mayhem, swilling beer, swapping stories, and partying with the wild and the weird.

If you partied too hard at Sturgis and feel the need for peace and tranquility, then head west back into Wyoming and Yellowstone, the world's first national park. It's a long 280-mile (450-km) ride, so consider breaking the journey at the town of Cody, and pay a visit to the excellent Buffalo Bill Center of the West. In addition to a museum dedicated to the man himself, there is a museum dedicated to the Plains Indians and the Cody Firearms Museum that are very interesting as well.

There are more than 310 miles (500 km) of roads within Yellowstone leading to canyons, cliffs, geysers, and hot springs. Enjoy the tranquility and breathtaking beauty of this magnificent landscape. From the southern border of Yellowstone, ride south for about 255 miles (410 km) through the Grand Teton National Park and skirt the edges of the Wind River Range. The stretch of road to Green River provides magnificent views of jagged, snow-capped peaks as well as great riding. Spend the night in the city of Green River, rising early to wind your way east past Flaming Gorge Reservoir and over the Uinta Mountains to Dinosaur National Monument, where you

The Million Dollar Highway en route to Durango, Colorado.

Riding past Mount Rushmore, South Dakota.

cross back into Colorado. Steamboat Springs makes a good overnight halt after a day's ride of about 275 miles (443 km). This is where the serious sport of motorcycling along mountainous passes really begins. There are dozens of passes to play on, so don't forget to stop occasionally and give your clutch a rest while you admire the peaks. Trail Ridge Road in the Rocky Mountain National Park, at more than 12,000 feet (3,650 m) in elevation and 47 miles (75 km) in length, is the highest continuous highway in the States. Ride high into an alpine world through mountain meadows, colorful tundra, and aspen groves. There are plenty of stopping points to admire the far-reaching views and snap pictures of you and your bike framed against a background of spectacular glaciers and snowfields.

From the Rocky Mountain National Park, drop back down to Denver for an overnight stop to check the tires and oil the clutch in anticipation of riding even more mountain passes. Leaving Denver, head west over the Loveland Pass, followed closely by the Fremont Pass, to the mountain town of Leadville and up over Independence Pass to Aspen.

If the glitz of Aspen is a little too much for you, then head northwest to Glenwood Springs for the night, where you can soak in the hot springs (approximately a 250-mile/402-km day's ride). From Glenwood Springs head southeast, skirting the north rim of the Black Canyon of the Gunnison and onto Ouray and the start of a ride along the "Million Dollar Highway" to Silverton. The ride through Uncompahgre Gorge to the summit of Red Mountain Pass consists of precipitous cliffs and hairpin bends as the road ascends the pass. Stay on the HW550 heading south to the town of Durango, a lively spot to pull over while your bike cools down and the tires stop steaming.

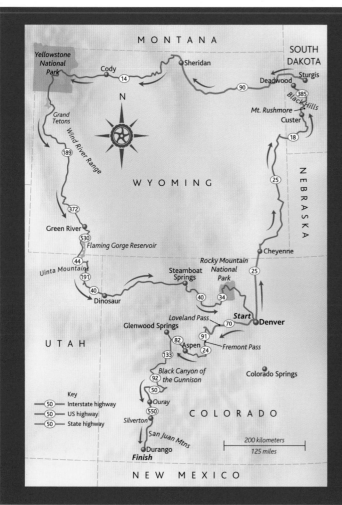

Bike: It is possible to take your own bike into the United States. Bike hire is available in Denver. There are operators offering bike-inclusive tours.

Weather Watch: June to mid-September is the best time to visit.

Extending the Ride: Ride west to the National Parks of Utah and Arizona or south to the Mexican border at El Paso.

Riding the roads around Sturgis.

The Grand Canyon National Park is well worth a few days' exploration.

USA

THE WILD WEST AND THE CALIFORNIAN COAST

Ride a circuit from Los Angeles through Arizona's Wild West, then across to Las Vegas in the Nevada desert. Head north to San Francisco, returning to Los Angeles via the Californian coast.

Grab the leading role in your own western and relive those classic John Wayne moments. Ride through Navajo and Apache lands, stop off at frontier towns, and gaze down on the grandest canyon of them all. Arizona, Utah, and Nevada represent America's west at its wildest. If names like Furnace Creek, Valley of the Gods, and Hell's Backbone light your imagination, then get your motor running and ride along roads that will have you grinning like Fonda and Hopper as you ride into the sunset.

Los Angeles makes a great starting point for a circular tour of switchbacks, sweeping curves, roads that disappear into the horizon, and jaw-dropping scenery, not to mention historic sections of Route 66 and the Pacific coastline of HW1. If you want to get off-road for some of the route, the Great Western Trail (*www.gwt.org*) is a corridor of parallel trails traversing over 1,864 miles (3,000 km) of canyons, deserts, woodlands, and forests, offering some truly adventurous riding. This region of the United States offers an extensive choice of riding terrains through incredible landscapes.

The Route

This route gives you a taste of the deserts of the Wild West, the glitz of Las Vegas, and the superb Californian coast. Two to three weeks will allow for time off the bike in the national parks.

Leave Los Angeles and head east, motoring along original sections of Route 66 as far as Williams, Arizona—the gateway to the Grand Canyon National Park. Nothing can prepare you for the soaring, spectacular beauty of this place. Stay a few days and hike into the canyon to get a feel of the scale and solitude of one of the world's natural wonders.

A 167-mile (270-km) ride east through the rocky landscape of the Painted Desert and into Navajo territory takes you to Monument Valley. This is where the west was won—at least in the movies. Its stark landscape, shifting red sands, and sandstone buttes with names such as The Mittens, Totem Pole, and Ear of the Wind has seen John Wayne and Clint Eastwood save the day, and no other place quite encapsulates our perception of the Wild West. A strange sense of déjà vu prevails as you gaze at these familiar landmarks silhouetted against a red evening sky. If you feel the need to hit the dirt, the trails created by 1950s uranium prospectors crisscross the area north of Monument Valley, and there are numerous options for great riding combined with spellbinding scenery in all directions.

Big Sur, where the Santa Lucia Mountains rise abruptly from the Pacific Ocean.

Leaving Monument Valley, head northwest to Bryce Canyon on HW276, which crosses the Colorado River to link up with an impressive road (HW24) that skirts the southern tip of Capital Reef National Park. Head south to Boulder City on HW12 and then take the ride of your life on a 38-mile (60-km) stretch across the top of the Aquarius Plateau. Hell's Backbone is a hair-raising ride with sheer drops to Sand Creek and Death Hollow on either side. The views are stupendous as the dirt road climbs up and around Box-Death Hollow Wilderness below and crosses a narrow bridge. At Escalante, return to HW12 and ride along a road blasted through the rocks to Bryce Canyon. As evening approaches, the changing light plays on the hoodoos (tall, thin spires of rock). This spectacle will allow you to experience an almost

above: Capitol Reef National Park, Utah.

far right: Yosemite National Park is famous for its spectacular granite cliffs, waterfalls, and giant sequoia groves.

psychedelic, Technicolor display of the weird and wonderful landscape, providing a magical end to an exhilarating day's ride. From here it is just over an hour's scenic ride to Zion National Park, a welcome oasis with its cascading waterfalls. Relax and wash off the desert dust in the cool waters on the Emerald Pools Trail.

Just 56 miles (90 km) southwest of Zion is Las Vegas, a city of fantasy shimmering in the desert. Enter the world of 24-hour entertainment, Elvis impersonators, and the infamous Las Vegas Strip. Once you've had your fill of fantasy, load up your bike and roar out of town in the early morning light into the Mojave Desert and Death Valley, descending below sea level into desolate and dramatic scenery. This is purportedly the hottest place on Earth, so slake your thirst at Furnace Creek and ride out to Dante's View before hitting the switchbacks and mountain passes leading north to Mammoth Lakes and Yosemite National Park. In Yosemite, ride over the Tioga Pass, which threads through alpine meadows along the spine of the Sierra Nevada.

A 186-mile (300-km) ride from Yosemite through Gold Country brings you to the beautiful city of San Francisco. Relax for a few days and appreciate its charms before hitting HW1 for the 400-mile (644-km) ride to Los Angeles. This is a fantastic finale to your journey through the Wild West. The coastal breeze will blow away the last of the desert sand as you cruise down a highway that hugs the rugged coast along the Pacific Ocean. Lighthouses, crumbling cliffs, soft white sand, and giant redwoods decorate the coastline. With a big, blue Californian sky above and a turquoise ocean as far as the eye can see, relax into the ride and enjoy some easy living. The surf is spectacular and there are enough sweeping curves and tight turns to keep the riding sweet until you swing into Los Angeles.

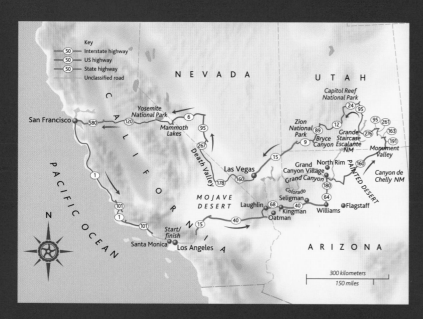

Bike: It is possible to take your own bike into the United States. Las Vegas, Los Angeles, and Phoenix all offer a wide choice of bike hire. There are operators offering bike-inclusive tours.

Weather Watch: The best time to visit is September to mid-October, or April and May for desert wildflowers. Avoid summer's baking desert temperatures.

Extending the Ride: From Los Angeles, follow Route 66 east as far as Albuquerque, then head north to Durango for a ride in the Colorado Rockies.

Los Angeles – the end of the road

USA

ROUTE 66: FLAGSTAFF TO LOS ANGELES

Route 66 crosses the country from Chicago to Los Angeles for 2,448 miles (3,939 km) through eight states. Many sections of the original road have been replaced by interstate highways, but it is still possible to follow much of the original road and, in doing so, relive a little of America's recent history.

Perhaps one of the most famous roads in the world, Route 66 has been immortalized in music, in literature, and on the screen. Fondly referred to as the Mother Road, it was established in 1926 and ran from Chicago to Los Angeles. In the 1930s, the road transported immigrants in search of a better life to sunny, golden California. By 1937 it was fully paved, becoming the main military route during WWII. In the 1950s, it was the road taken by vacationers heading to the West Coast. Roadside attractions and fast-food joints sprang up along the way to cater to the passing trade, until eventually the road itself became part of the vacation. Although officially decommissioned in 1985, the spirit of the road in its heyday lives on.

This motorcycle journey is not about negotiating hairpin bends or climbing high for spectacular views; in fact, much of the original highway was flat. It is more a journey into a state of mind, a motorcycle ride through history following a road that represented freedom and adventure. Whatever your preferred bike, perhaps, just this once, a Harley Davidson is the motorcycle to ride on this celebrated route. Ride an American machine as you follow the road that epitomizes the American Dream.

The Route

Riding the full length of Route 66 would probably take about three weeks. The following route can be ridden in a couple of days and covers the final section from Flagstaff, Arizona, to Los Angeles, California, along some of the best-surviving stretches of the original road where classic gas stations, motels, and diners evoke everything you have ever heard about this classic route.

above: Motorcycle journeys in the United States can be epic in scale, so take frequent breaks and enjoy the ride.

below: The iconic Route 66, which historically ran from Chicago to LA.

Pick up a hire-bike in Phoenix, then head north on Interstate 17 for about 140 miles (225 km) to Flagstaff. About 25 miles (40 km) west of Flagstaff is the town of Williams, gateway to the Grand Canyon, and, historically, the last town to have its section of the Mother Road bypassed. Park at one of the classic 1950s diners or try an ice cream soda at Twisters Soda Fountain.

A short ride west brings you to the village of Ash Fork and the start of about 162 miles (260 km) of the original Route 66. Open up the throttle as you motor across open plains to Seligman, another classic Route 66 town and a must stop on your ride. Seligman is home to Angel Delgadillo, the founding member of the association to preserve the Mother Road. Known as the "Angel of Route 66," his barbershop/gift shop walls are lined with business cards and stickers from passing clients, ones who perhaps hoped for a change of image to complement their new life. His brother Juan passed away in 2004, but his famous Snow Cap Drive-In is still run by the family.

Continuing west, the road dips through rolling countryside, affording expansive views. This is the open road, and the Harley is in its element, that familiar throaty rumble of the engine filling the air. Fill up at the gas station at Hackberry, its forecourt a colorful reminder of 1950s America. Southwest of Kingman, the road starts to climb into the Black Mountains and the most enjoyable riding of the route. Ease on that lazy Harley power and glide along the narrow road as it snakes and twists through the mountains, climbing through canyons towards Oatman. Once a gold-mining center, these days the dusty streets are filled with creaky saloons and roaming donkeys.

From Oatman, the road descends toward Topock and the Californian border. The cool mountains give way to a dry heat and dramatic landscape as you approach Los Angeles through the Mojave Desert. Cruise into town and head for the Santa Monica Pier. Cut the engine, gaze across the Pacific Ocean, and reflect on your once-in-a-lifetime ride along this iconic road.

Old gas pumps along Route 66.

Bike: It is possible to take your own bike into the United States. Bike hire is available in Phoenix and Los Angeles. There are operators offering bike-inclusive tours.

Weather Watch: May to September is the best time to visit.

Extending the Ride: Incorporate this ride into a trip through Arizona's Wild West.

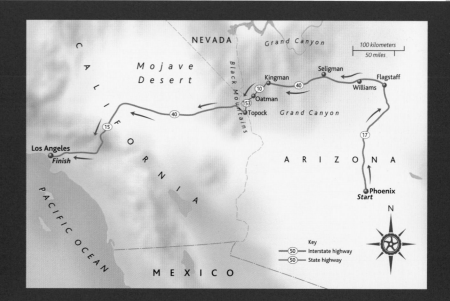

Cacti in northern Mexico.

MEXICO

THE SIERRA MADRE MOUNTAINS TO THE BAJA PENINSULA

Ride from the Rio Grande across the Chihuahua Desert through the canyons of the Sierra Madre Mountains and over the Devil's Backbone to the warm waters of the Pacific Coast, where you'll ferry over to the Baja Peninsula.

Northern Mexico is a region of mountains, desert, giant cacti, and sleepy, dusty towns where spicy tortillas are washed down with tequila and mustachioed mariachi bands play at weeklong fiestas. Folklore and magic rituals interweave with the Catholicism of the conquistadors, and the history of the region echoes with stories of the Mexican Revolution. The Baja Peninsula offers mountains, beaches, and up-close encounters with whales. The skies are brilliant blue, the beer is cold, and the welcome from the Mexican people is warm and inviting.

The motorcycling possibilities are endless, and you will be amazed by the varied terrain and choice of riding. You can cruise the highways on a sports bike; the toll roads are expensive but well surfaced and fast; or take a dual sport machine and brave the dirt roads, canyon descents, and river crossings to really get a flavor of Mexico's natural beauty.

The Route

This route can be ridden in a week. Allow a bit longer if you plan to include some sightseeing.

Crossing into Mexico over the Rio Grande from El Paso, Texas, you hit the arid, rocky deserts of Mexico's north, the landscape characterized by giant Saguaro cacti and, after the summer rains, stunning desert wildflowers. A fast five-hour ride south through the desert on HW45 brings you to the city of Chihuahua, synonymous with the Mexican Revolution and the life of Mexico's hero Pancho Villa. His home is now the Museo de la Revolución Mexicana.

It is a fun, twisting 143 miles (230 km) south along HW16 to Creel, a mountain town perched at 7,546 feet (2,300 m) and surrounded by pine-covered mountains. Creel makes a good base for visiting the incredible Copper Canyon. The name is given to the network of mammoth canyons that cut through the Sierra Madre range and which are even larger than the Grand Canyon in the United States. This world-famous canyon system is one of Mexico's natural wonders and will be a highlight of your ride through Mexico. As dirt roads are upgraded, an increasing network of paved roads now connects the canyons. Dirt bikers can enjoy the off-road trails and road bikes can follow the 31-mile (50-km) paved road running along the rim of Cooper Canyon from Creel to El Divisadero. Lodges perch on the edge of the canyon, offering truly spectacular views. Stay the night to experience the stunning sunset and the enveloping silence.

There are six separate canyons in the Copper Canyon system.

You can leave your bike for a few days and trek into the canyon, or ride the road to the former mining village of Batopilas, which lies at the bottom. It is a thrilling 193-mile (150-km) ride from Creel on a partly paved but mainly dirt road that switchbacks and twists its way to the ravine below, descending nearly 5,000 feet (1,500 m) through dramatic scenery. Depending on your off-road experience, it can take three to six hours to complete the descent. At 1,624 feet (495 m), Batopilas's climate is distinctly warmer; tropical fruit thrives there and the streets are lined with bougainvillea.

above: Durango was once a popular location for shooting movies.

far right: Finding a shady spot en route to the coast at Mazatlán.

The same road climbs out of the canyon to Creel, where you head south for about 100 miles (150 km) to Guachochi along a road that skirts the edge of the canyons, continuing for a further 119 miles (190 km) on HW23 through cactus-strewn mountain scenery to Hidalgo del Parral, infamous as the site of Pancho Villa's assassination. A brief stay is recommended to enjoy this charming, mellow town with narrow, winding streets.

Join HW45 for the fast 255-mile (410-km) ride to Durango, a cowboy town and once a popular movie location. There are plenty of hotels and restaurants, and the leafy square is a great place to pull over and sit in the shade near the cool fountains.

Head southwest from Durango to Mazatlán on the Pacific Coast. The spectacular stretch of road called El Espinazo del Diablo (Devil's Backbone) was once the only route through the Sierra Madre Mountains. The highway bypass was completed in 2013 and will take you all the way south of the Tropic of Cancer to the palm-fringed beaches of Mazatlán. From here, pick up a ferry across the Gulf of California (Sea of Cortez) to La Paz on the Baja Peninsula. Beautiful beaches line the stretch of coast between Cabo San Lucas and San José del Cabo on the southern tip. Time your visit between December and

March to catch the migration of gray whales from Arctic waters to the sheltered lagoons of Baja, where they breed and rear their young. Getting up close to these gentle and magnificent giants is the perfect way to end your Mexican motorcycle adventure.

Bike: It is possible to take your own bike into Mexico. Bike hire in San Antonio, Texas, or Phoenix, Arizona, is recommended. There are operators offering bike-inclusive tours into Mexico from Texas.

Weather Watch: It is a year-round destination, but expect chilly nights from November to February and rain from May to October.

Extending the Ride: Ride north to Phoenix, where you can join the final section of Route 66 or take a ride through Arizona's Wild West.

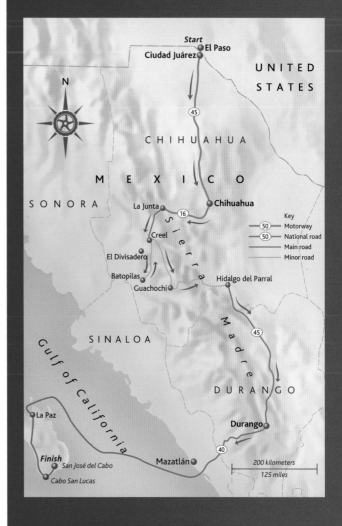

The Arenal Volcano is still active and last had a major eruption in 2000.

COSTA RICA

SAN JOSÉ TO CORDILLERA DE GUANACASTE

Ride north from San José through the lush Central Valley, then head across to the idyllic beaches of the Nicoya Peninsula before heading north toward Nicaragua.

Tiny Costa Rica is Central America made simple; a safe and peaceful paradise bordered by the warm waters of the Pacific and the Caribbean. Costa Rica's uniqueness lies in its variety of landscapes, climate zones, and incredibly colorful wildlife. Howler monkeys and flamboyant parakeets screech from the trees, giant lizards sunbathe on the rock-strewn roads, and tiny hummingbirds, magnificent butterflies, and iridescent frogs enthrall visitors to the national parks. Relax on tropical beaches where the rainforest spills onto the sand, step into an enchanted world on canopy walks that swing through the cloud forest, and watch in awe as active volcanoes illuminate the night sky.

Distances are relatively short; nowhere is more than a long day's ride from the capital. The road network is extensive but varied, with short stretches of dual-lane roads leading out of the capital which then branch off to single-track, potholed roads and gravel trails. It is possible to stick to a combination of highways and paved roads, just occasionally tackling a dirt road. Alternatively, spend the whole journey ripping along the network of single trails, tackling a challenging combination of dirt, sand, and gravel, with the occasional river crossing and swaying suspension bridge thrown in to add to the fun. The weather can be unpredictable, so pack for rain and follow the good weather, as sudden tropical downpours can quickly turn the trails to mud. Riding in Costa Rica is fantastic fun, and the choice of riding terrain is entirely up to you.

The Route

This classic one-week route connects some of Costa Rica's most famous highlights, riding a mixture of paved and dirt roads.

above: Make sure you leave time to enjoy Costa Rica's idyllic beaches.

above left: Jungle river crossing.

above right: Gravel roads lead to the Pacific Ocean.

From San José, head northwest (HW1PAH) through the Central Valley to the town of Alajuela. The views are stunning as the small, paved road climbs through fruit farms and coffee plantations up the slopes of the Poás Volcano, just 22 miles (35 km) north of Alajuela. Poás is an active volcano, and you can walk along a path that leads around the crater rim for views into its steaming lagoon.

Continue northwest for about 100 miles (150 km) via narrow, paved roads that wind through gorgeous valleys to Fortuna, gateway to the Arenal National Park and the Arenal Volcano, a classic cone-shaped active volcano that regularly emits rock bombs and fiery orange lava. There are ample places to stay in the area, so unpack the bike and join one of the late-afternoon treks through the rainforest, concluding in an evening bath in the Tabacón hot springs. Lounge in the thermal waters, listen to the volcanic rumblings, and watch the nighttime display.

From Fortuna, head west along the R142, a bumpy road that skirts around the northern edge of Lake Arenal for 25 miles (40 km) to Tilarán, where you pick up a rough dirt road (R145) for a further 25 miles (40 km) to the beautiful cloud forest reserve of Monteverde. Road conditions get rough—loose gravel with some big rocks—but the views over mountains and valleys are stupendous. There is plenty of accommodation and amenities at the nearby town of Santa Elena, where you can pick up a bus to the Monteverde Reserve. Spend at least a day on the marked walking trails exploring the luxuriant

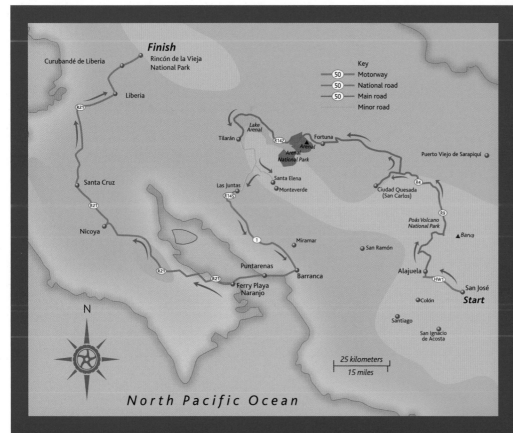

Bike: It is possible to take your own bike into Costa Rica. Bike hire is available in San José. There are operators offering bike-inclusive tours.

Weather Watch: December to mid-May is the dry season. Rains are heaviest in June and October, but be prepared for rain at any time.

Extending the Ride: No overland connection to other featured journeys.

vegetation at Monteverde, which is home to an astounding variety of wildlife. Stroll across suspended walkways for a monkey's eye view of the steaming rainforest, or opt for a thrilling zip-line ride.

Leaving Monteverde, it is a full day's ride of about 99 miles (160 km) to the coast. Some 22 miles (35 km) of challenging, twisting dirt roads and spectacular views await you on the R145 before you pick up the Pan-American Highway near the town of Las Juntas. Head south, branching off at Barranca toward the port of Puntarenas to pick up the ferry to the Nicoya Peninsula, which takes about an hour. Roll off the ferry and head for one of the many small beach resorts along the coast. Find yourself a base for a few days, off-load the luggage, and take to the inland trails of the peninsula

on your bike for some challenging riding on sandy tracks. From the town of Nicoya, pick up R21 heading north and connect with the Pan-American Highway at Liberia. Continue north, turning off the highway and onto an unpaved rocky trail to Curubandé de Liberia for the last 12 miles (20 km) to the little-visited Rincón de la Vieja National Park, where lava and hot mud boil under the surface of this stunning, surreal landscape dominated by the dramatic Rincón de la Vieja Volcano. Take a break from the riding, leave

your bike at one of the park's lodges, and hike to the summit for views that take in the Nicoya Peninsula and extend to neighboring Nicaragua. This is the beauty of riding in Costa Rica—short distances, constantly changing scenery, and a fun, varied choice of riding terrain.

Enjoying the view from the Monteverde road.

Near the Chile/Argentina border.

CHILE/ARGENTINA

PATAGONIA: JOURNEY TO THE END OF THE WORLD

Ride from Temuco in Chile to Ushuaia, the capital of the Argentinean province of Tierra del Fuego, and the world's southernmost city.

Riding down through Patagonia to Tierra del Fuego at the tip of South America, it can really feel like you are approaching the end of the Earth. While the northern part is a land of lakes and snow-capped peaks with an almost European, alpine appearance, as you travel southwards the scenery and weather become wilder and population centers smaller and further apart. Eventually you reach Ushuaia in Argentina—*el fin del mundo*—and after that it's just Cape Horn and Antarctica. Patagonia is the area of South America lying below 37 degrees south and consists of both Chilean and Argentinean territory. You will find yourself crossing the two frontiers many times, but the route is very straightforward with few delays at customs. Campsites and inexpensive hotels are easily found along the route.

The Andes run the whole length of the western side of South America, and you will cross back and forth over them many times on your journey—one of the highlights as the twisting roads take you from one side to the other. Then you come to the famous Route 40 (Ruta 40)—hundreds of miles of gravel road where you can be blown off course and buffeted constantly by the strong winds sweeping across Patagonia. You will soon get used to riding your bike leaning at an angle. It is possible to avoid sections of this road and keep to more sealed routes if you wish. Although riding in this region is reasonably straightforward, don't underestimate the time it will take to complete your journey on the unpaved roads, and always top off your tank where you can as rural gas stations close in the early evening.

The Route

The drive will take you two to three weeks to complete, allowing time for sightseeing and breaks from riding.

Begin your journey in Temuco in Chilean Patagonia, an area known as the "Lake District." Heading southeast toward the Andes, it is a short ride of 70 miles (112 km) to the towns of Villarrica and Pucón, the start of a region of huge lakes and snow-capped volcanoes. Pucón is a center for adventure activities, so accommodation options are plentiful. The smooth, paved road twists its way alongside a deep blue lake with the Volcán Villarrica as your backdrop. It is possible to walk up this snowy peak and peer down into its

The Perito Moreno Glacier is still advancing.

crater, the glowing lava and sulfurous smoke rising up toward you. Travel on good dirt roads past giant pine forests and lakes in the Villarrica National Park for 54 miles (87 km) to the Argentinean border.

Heading down the other side of the mountains, you will ride on a combination of dirt and sealed roads which will take you past many scenic lakes. Stay overnight at San Martín de los Andes, or the resort of Bariloche. The last 12 miles (20 km) of your ride hugs the shore of Nahuel Huapi Lake. Bariloche itself is a very Swiss-looking town and ski resort beautifully situated on the shore of the lake, and it is the center for outdoor activities. From here, the winding and narrow sealed road heads south for about 160 miles (260 km),

The Patagonian Lake District in Chile, where this journey begins.

running past more stunning scenery, which then opens up into rolling hills as you approach the town of Esquel, a hub for visits into the Los Alerces National Park. The last 62 miles (100 km) are on the infamous Route 40, and it can be extremely windy, so be careful not to get blown off the road. You really feel like you are in wild Patagonia from here on down; southward from here, the roads are entirely gravel or dirt embedded with rocks. The Andes will be to your right from now on and contain the largest glaciers outside the polar region. This is the land of the *gauchos* (cowboys), where the only indication of habitation is signs by the entrance roads to huge *estancias* (cattle farms). Keep your wheels running inside the ruts in the gravel left by other vehicles and try to avoid being blown into the pile of stones along the center, which is often several inches deep.

There are some great side trips not to be missed on the way down. Once you reach Tres Lagos, 323 miles (520 km) south of Chile Chico, turn off Route 40 and take a dirt road for about 93 miles (150 km) to the small settlement of El Chaltén in the Los Glaciares National Park. From here, short treks are possible to see stupendous views of Mt. Fitz Roy and Cerro Torre.

Return back to the junction and turn off after 62 miles (100 km) to El Calafate. From there you can ride down to see the immense Perito Moreno

Glacier, one of the few in the world that is actually advancing. You can stand and watch large pieces of ice fall away from the 3-mile (5-km) wide snout and plunge into the vivid blue lake.

Retrace your route back to join Route 40 and head back south for 124 miles (200 km) through Cerro Castillo to Puerto Natales in Chile. You will see guanacos (a relative of the llama), possibly condors, and even flamingos on the salt flats near the border. It is well worth riding into the Torres del Paine National Park along a good dirt road with truly wonderful views of the Torres themselves and the Cuernos del Paine towering above the lake as you ride around the opposite bank. Torres del Paine is one of South America's greatest national parks.

Cut back east to ride 124 miles (200 km) across desolate, windswept pampas back into Argentina, passing old, ruined settlements to reach the town of Río Gallegos and the end of Route 40. From here you need to take Route 3. Head south, cross back into Chile, and take the ferry the short distance over the Strait of Magellan to the island of Tierra del Fuego. The island is divided between both Argentina and Chile and is a wild land of stunning lakes, forests, and mountain scenery. From the ferry, you can see your final destination—the Argentinean town of Ushuaia—280 miles (450 km) away. The town is situated on the Beagle Channel; Charles Darwin named the channel after his ship in 1832. The town is a departure point for ships to Antarctica and can be quite busy when they are in port. There is only one last thing to do at the end of your long ride. Travel a few miles out of town to the end of the road until you can go no further. After some long, tough riding, you have finally reached the end of the world.

Bike: It is possible to take your own bike into Chile. You can hire bikes in Osorno. There are operators offering bike-inclusive tours.

Weather Watch: December to March is really the only time to ride this route by motorcycle.

Extending the Ride: No overland connection to other featured journeys.

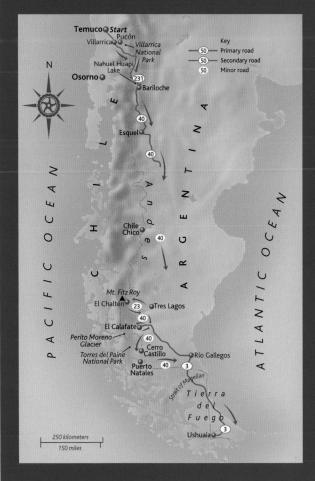

ASIA

Baralacha La, on the Manali to Leh road.

Buddhist cave temples at Dambulla.

SRI LANKA

COLOMBO CIRCUIT

Ride north from Colombo to the Cultural Triangle, dropping slightly south to the central hill country before returning to Colombo on roads that wind through tea plantations.

The island of Sri Lanka is a beautiful paradise of idyllic beaches, thick jungles, and highlands swathed with tea plantations. Ancient Buddhist art can be found in cave temples and ancient cities, while the colossal rock fortress at Sigiriya rises from the rainforest, affording spectacular views. Sri Lanka is wonderful for wildlife lovers. There are numerous national parks, the most famous of which is Yala, home of the elusive leopard. Elephants are everywhere, and if you time your visit right, you may even catch the migration of the blue whale. The landscape is stunning and the cuisine is unique and delicious, but it is the warm welcome and genuine kindness of the Sri Lankan people that will stay with you long after leaving the "Island of Serendipity."

Traveling by motorcycle has to be one of the best ways to appreciate the gorgeous scenery here. The road surfaces are not great and potholes litter even the main roads, but the pace of traffic is fairly slow and a 250cc bike is quite adequate and suits the pace. Distances between places of interest are short, and if you want to blow the budget, there are some fabulous places to stay. This is a relaxed motorcycle trip where you can ride for a day through lovely countryside, find a tranquil base, and spend a few days exploring the surrounding area.

The Route

Ten days for the following route allows for a two- to three-night stay in each region.

Get an early start out of Colombo before the traffic gets too frantic. The 91-mile (148-km) ride north to Dambulla, at the heart of the Cultural Triangle, is short, but the main two-lane highway (A1/A6) is busy and uneven in places as the road winds through a verdant countryside of paddy fields, banana plantations, and coconut palms. Dambulla makes a good base for exploring the sights of the Cultural Triangle, which is littered with the remains of ancient palaces and cities. Don't be too surprised if you see wild elephants wandering across the road—it goes without saying that they have the right of way! At Dambulla, visit the Buddhist cave temples, then take a short 14-mile (25-km) ride north to the magnificent 5th-century citadel of Sigiriya. Designated a UNESCO World Heritage Site in 1982, it towers above the plains atop a 656-foot (200-m) rocky outcrop, and a climb of about 1,500 steps takes you to the summit for far-reaching views.

The following day, take a 42-mile (68-km) ride to the ancient capital of Polonnaruwa, where temples, palaces, and sculptures lay hidden in the surrounding woodland. You can rent bicycles in the town to transport you

A tea plantation near Nuwara Eliya.

around this huge site. Leaving the Cultural Triangle, head southeast on the A9 toward Kandy and the hill country. Run the gauntlet of spice merchants whose gardens line the road near Matale, then drop down through green hills to the lovely lakeside city of Kandy, another great base for a few days. Visit the temple that houses Sri Lanka's most important Buddhist relic, Buddha's Tooth, ride out to the botanical gardens, and take a day trip to the Pinnawala Elephant Orphanage just 25 miles (40 km) west of Kandy. Their bath time in the Maha Oya River is not to be missed.

Leaving Kandy, the 47-mile (77-km) ride (A5) into the hill country is incredibly scenic but also unforgettably bumpy, making the ride fairly slow going. Break the journey with a visit to one of the tea estates you will pass

along the way. Stay for the after-tour tea and cake, or spend the night at one of the converted factories. Step back in time as you approach the old British hill town of Nuwara Eliya, where you can stay in hotels that appear little changed since the turn of the century. This is the heart of the tea industry, and the surrounding countryside is beautiful. Take a scenic 19-mile (30-km) ride out to Horton Plains National Park, a rugged, high-altitude moorland where the dramatic escarpment of World's End plunges through mists to the plains. If you want to stretch your legs, there are some great walks within the park that you can easily do in a day.

From Nuwara Eliya, weave your way back to Colombo along possibly the most stunning road of the trip, the A7, which winds for 111 miles (180 km) through lush forest and tea plantations, every turn revealing breathtaking views. Spend your last evening in Sri Lanka strolling along Galle Face Green, the oceanfront promenade, which is alive with street food vendors and families enjoying the balmy ocean breeze.

above: Kandy is one of the most scenic cities in Sri Lanka.

below: Exploring the dirt roads in Sri Lanka.

Outside a Hindu temple in Negombo, just north of Colombo.

Bike: Getting your own bike into Sri Lanka is not straightforward as there is no land route. Limited bike hire is available in Negombo, generally offering smaller-capacity engines, but they are ideal for this terrain. There are operators offering bike-inclusive tours.

Weather Watch: December to April is the best time to visit, but expect rain at any time of the year.

Extending the Ride: No overland connection to other featured journeys.

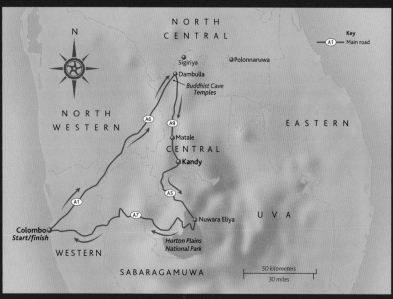

The camel fair in Pushkar.

INDIA

DELHI TO JAISALMER

From Delhi, take a ride through the state of Rajasthan to Jaisalmer in the Great Thar Desert.

The desert state of Rajasthan is the India of sandstone fortresses, architecturally intricate *havalis* (enclosed dwellings), turbaned and mustachioed men, and beautiful, brightly dressed tribal women. For extremes of color against a sparse desert landscape, and as in introduction to the Indian subcontinent, Rajasthan is hard to beat. Many of the fabulously wealthy Maharajas that once ruled much of northern India have turned their palaces into hotels, so consider blowing the budget and spending at least one night in a converted palace.

Riding in India is a nerve-jangling, death-defying experience and not for the faint-hearted. Size really does matter on Indian roads, so be prepared to pull onto the dirt to let oncoming trucks go past or to avoid sleeping cows. Riding in India is both great fun and an emotional roller coaster—tears of frustration can turn to laughter in minutes, as there is always something to make you smile. The people you meet and the things you see ensure there will never be a dull day's ride. Traffic, livestock, and humanity compete for space in the cities but, once out on the open road, rural India is magical. If you are picking up a bike in India, it has to be the Royal Enfield Bullet, a classic motorcycle designed in the 1950s and still produced in Madras. The brakes are poor and the suspension basic, but spares and mechanics are widespread and the pace, sound, and feel is perfectly in tune with the surroundings. The Bullet is temperamental, indestructible, and in her element on the Indian roads.

The Route

Allow two weeks for this journey as there is much to see, and a ride in India is so much more enjoyable if you are not in a rush; the fun of riding in India is the journey itself.

above: Palace of the Winds, Jaipur.

Enfield Bullet, Jaisalmer.

As with any journey in India, try to leave early when the air is cool and the country is slowly awakening, so ride out of Delhi at first light before the traffic mayhem begins. The 162-mile (260-km) run southwest to Jaipur is along a fairly fast, busy road littered with potholes, so you'll need to have your wits about you. Lorries and buses career past, belching diesel fumes in their wake, and your sooty face will amuse hotel-owners throughout your journey.

Spend your first few nights in the pink city of Jaipur, visiting the myriad palaces, temples, and bazaars in and around the city. It's only about 9 miles (15

km) out of the city along a scenic road to the impressive 16th-century Amer Fort, making for a great day's ride. As with any road journey in India, always get to your hotel before dusk, as the lack of streetlights and the burning of paraffin stoves make riding at dusk a dangerous experience.

It is just under 93 miles (150 km) west to Pushkar, but average speeds are low on India's rural roads. Throughout your journey there will always be a chai stand by the side of the road offering sweet tea and respite from the heat and dust. Another favorite are the omelette stands, great for a mid-morning snack if

above: Mehrangarh Fort, Jodhpur.

below: A chai stand in the Great Thar Desert.

you got on the road at dawn, but watch out for the chilies! Try to visit Pushkar in November when it hosts the annual Camel Fair. Rajasthani villagers travel in droves to the town, bringing camels and livestock to sell and race. Women leave their homes dressed in their finest clothes to buy bangles and silks and to visit the temples. It is an amazing experience where you can witness scorpion-swallowing magicians, an Indian "wall of death" ride, and, of course, camel racing.

From Pushkar, it is a dusty 124-mile (200-km) ride southwest to Jodhpur on the fringe of the Great Thar Desert, and you will probably be sharing the road

with camel and buffalo carts. Jodhpur is dominated by the mighty Mehrangarh Fort. Get up onto the ramparts for far-reaching views over the blue and white houses of the city and to the desert beyond. From Jodhpur, head 186 miles (300 km) west to Jaisalmer in India's remote western corner. It is a long, hot, dusty ride, but the final approach to Jaisalmer is a spectacular sight as the honey-colored sandstone ramparts of Jaisalmer Fort rise out of the desert plains. Lose yourself in the narrow streets, join a camel trek, and take a 28-mile (45-km) ride out to the sand dunes at

Sam on the edge of the Thar Desert, almost on the India-Pakistan border. India is a riding experience like no other, requiring concentration, patience, and, above all, a sense of humor. Hang on to this and you will have the ride of your life.

above left: There's always room for one more!

above right: Jewel-colored saris glow against the dusty land.

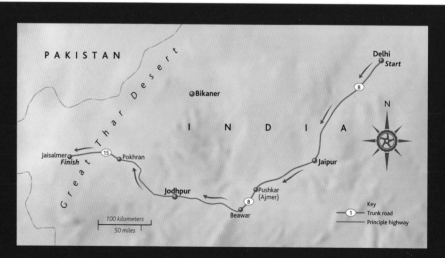

Bike: It is possible to take your own bike into India. Bike hire or buy-back schemes, especially for the Bullet, are available in Delhi. There are operators offering bike-inclusive tours.

Weather Watch: November to February is the best time to visit. Avoid summer's baking temperatures.

Extending the Ride: From Delhi ride north to Ladakh.

PAKISTAN

Great Thar Desert

Bikaner

I N D I A

Delhi
Start

8

N

Jaisalmer
Finish
15
Pokhran

Jaipur

Jodhpur

Pushkar
(Ajmer)
8
Beawar

Key
1 — Trunk road
— Principle highway

100 kilometers
50 miles

The Gata Loops, a series of spectacular hairpins.

INDIA

MANALI TO LEH

Ride from Manali in the fertile valleys of Himachal Pradesh, through remote valleys and onto the Tibetan Plateau, and finally to Leh, in the Kingdom of Ladakh.

Perched on the northern tip of India, this Shangri-La of Tibetan Buddhism nestles between the towering mountain ranges of the Himalaya and the Karakorum. Once an important crossroads on the Silk Route between central and southeast Asia, Ladakh was closed to foreigners until 1974. These days the weather conditions seal Ladakh from the outside world until the summer months, when the snow is cleared and we are allowed a glimpse of this legendary land. It is now possible to ride to this remote and beautiful mountain kingdom on the legendary Leh-Manali Highway. Your incredible journey will take you past snow-capped peaks and ancient Lamaist monasteries clinging to sheer rock faces. It is a rollercoaster of a ride through a beautiful and austere landscape. Hairpin bends wind skyward over the high-altitude passes you must traverse to reach the fabled city of Leh. The road is single-track, and road conditions differ from year to year as extreme weather conditions take their toll. Landslides and broken bridges are common and potholes fill with water and mud, but it is one of the most scenic roads in the world and is an unforgettable experience.

The Route

The road from Manali to Leh is one of the world's highest drivable roads and weaves for almost 311 miles (500 km) over 13,123-foot (4,000-m) passes. The following journey includes two overnight stops, allowing time to enjoy the riding and acclimatize to the high altitudes.

The mountain town of Manali is a melting pot of Indian honeymooners, high-altitude trekkers, and high-as-a-kite hippies. Explore the markets, stock up on warm clothes and supplies, check your bike,

above: Divine intervention!

above: The Indus Valley and the Ladakh Range.

below: Prayer flags are a common sight in this corner of the world.

and fill up the tank before you start out on this epic journey. As you ride out of town, imaginative road signs ask you to "be gentle on my curves" and advise road users, "Darling, I want you, but not so fast." The road instantly starts to climb through stunning Himalayan scenery shrouded by mountain mist. The air gets sharper and thinner and the backdrop becomes more barren as you approach the Rohtang La Pass (13,051 feet/3,978 m), just over an hour's ride from Manali. Early in the season, a wall of snow cleared from the road forms a tunnel through the pass. At Rohtang La, pull over to admire the stupendous view of the summits of Spiti and check your brakes before the road plunges into the Chandra Valley and the landscape changes to a stark, barren beauty. Tibetan prayer flags appear by the roadside and monasteries beckon from distant mountains as you motor the length of the valley. Top off the tank at the village of Tandi, the only fuel pump on the route.

At about 78 miles (125 km) from Manali, the town of Keylong is the main administrative center for the Lahaul and Spiti district. There are accommodation options, plus it is close to the famous 12th-century Kardang

Monastery, which sits just north of the town against a mountainous backdrop. The Shashur Gompa and Tayul Gompa are also located nearby, so extend your journey with an overnight stay to visit these very special Buddhist sites. It is a tough ride up and over the 16,049-foot (4,892-m) Baralacha La Pass. Rain can wash away road surfaces, so be prepared to tackle dirt tracks, rocks, boulders, and chilly mountain streams on the road ahead. Views of the Himalaya are, at these altitudes, literally breathtaking, so take it slowly as you acclimatize. Spend the night at the tented camp at Sarchu, about 93 miles (150 km) from Keylong, waking refreshed for the next enjoyable section.

The 21 switchbacks of the Gata Loops rise through a lunar landscape in a series of spectacular hairpins toward the Nakila and Lungalacha La 16,597-foot (5,059-m) passes. Give the engine a rest and cut the switch as you freewheel down from the passes through a wind-eroded landscape. From the military post at Pang, the tarred road rises for about 25 miles (40 km) to the high-altitude Mori Plains on the Tibetan Plateau. Surrounded by glacial peaks, this wide valley is often used by nomads to graze their yaks. The area is rich in wildlife, including the kyang (wild ass), red fox, and elusive snow leopard. Only the Tanglang La Pass—the world's second-highest drivable pass at 17,470 feet (5,325 m)—lies between you and the Indus Valley. The pass affords panoramic views of the Karakoram Mountains before descending in hairpin bends to the lovely Miru Gorge. Villages start to appear in patches of green pasture and monasteries perch on the hillsides, adding color. Ride into Ladkah's capital Leh, having completed one of the world's classic rides. Situated at 11,500 feet (3,505 m), Leh sprawls at the foot of a ruined Tibetan-style palace. Relax for a few days in this beautiful city, as the highest drivable pass is still to come!

The Khardung La is the gateway to the lush, green Nubra Valley. The pass is situated about 23 miles (37 km) by road from Leh. The first 15 miles (24 km), as far as the first checkpoint, are paved. From there the road is mainly loose rock, dirt, and occasional snowmelt. This superb feat of engineering winds to an incredible 18,389 feet (5,605 m). The views from the pass to the mountains of Tibet, the Karakoram Range, and the Indus Valley are awe-inspiring; your sense of achievement as you stand next to your bike is immense.

Bike: It is possible to take your own bike into India. Bike hire or buy-back schemes are available in Delhi or Manali. There are operators offering bike-inclusive tours.

Weather Watch: Subject to weather conditions, the road is only open from July to early October.

Extending the Ride: From Manali, it is about 373 miles (600 km) to Delhi for the start of a ride around Rajasthan.

The picturesque town of Mae Hong Son.

THAILAND

CHIANG MAI TO GOLDEN TRIANGLE LOOP

Ride the Mae Hong Son Loop, head north to the Golden Triangle, and return to Chiang Mai via remote eastern provinces.

Sleepy roads wind through mist-shrouded rainforests, weave through lush tropical jungles, and trundle through tranquil villages. This is a country renowned for its outstanding natural beauty, distinctive culture, and beautiful smiles. The towns and villages strung along the Mekong River and the Burmese (Myanmar) and Laos borders are home to Thailand's colorful hill-tribe people. Mountain trails abound, leading to mystical temples, golden Buddhas, and the ruins of ancient cities.

Riding in northern Thailand is relatively undemanding, entertaining, and great fun. In general, highway signage is in English. Rural roads meander past paddy fields, over forested mountain passes, and along tropical jungle trails. The distances are short and roads generally quiet. Open-air restaurants serve culinary delights and are very much part of the Thai road trip, as are the beautiful and inexpensive lodges. For those wanting to up the challenge a little, river crossings, log bridges, ruts, and slippery slopes offer exciting off-road possibilities. Northern Thailand's network of roads and off-road trails, combined with fantastic food and accommodation, make for a wonderful introduction to riding in Asia.

The Route

The following circuit will take you about two weeks if combined with sightseeing and a few days of trekking.

The Mae Hong Son Loop is a well-known network of on- and off-road trails southwest and northwest of the city of Chiang Mai, Thailand's northern capital. Roads run through a wild hill country of tropical and teak forests, rugged limestone karsts, and densely forested slopes. The

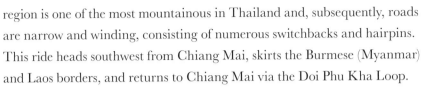

above: The Golden Triangle, where Thailand, Burma, and Laos meet.

below: Taking a break on the Mae Hong Son Loop.

region is one of the most mountainous in Thailand and, subsequently, roads are narrow and winding, consisting of numerous switchbacks and hairpins. This ride heads southwest from Chiang Mai, skirts the Burmese (Myanmar) and Laos borders, and returns to Chiang Mai via the Doi Phu Kha Loop.

From Chiang Mai, take HW108 southwest to Mae Chaem for the start of a great ride of thrilling switchbacks to the summit of Doi Inthanon, Thailand's highest peak. Then ride north on the challenging Route 1263 to the sleepy town of Khun Yuam. It is a further 53 miles (85 km) north to the town of Mae Hong Son, located in a valley ringed by forested mountains. From Mae Hong Son, the 75-mile (120-km) loop to Pai winds through an area of forests, rugged mountains, and limestone caves, offering truly fabulous riding. Route 1095 is a highlight of a ride in this area and a favorite with local bikers. The road winds over mountain trails and through gorgeous green paddy fields. Tight, gravel-strewn corners can catch the unwary, so pull over if you want to admire the scenery.

Pai and Chiang Dao are both major trekking centers. If you want to stretch your legs, take a climb toward the summit of Doi Chiang Dao, which reaches 7,136 feet (2,175 m). At the base of the mountain is a *wat* (Buddhist temple), marking the entrance to one of Thailand's deepest limestone caverns with more than 40 feet (12 m) of stalactite-covered tunnels to explore.

Continue north on Route 107 to Tha Ton, a 71-mile (115-km) ride from Chiang Dao. You are now entering the Golden Triangle, the meeting point of Thailand, Burma (Myanmar), and Laos. This area was once synonymous with opium growing and drug smuggling; although those days are long gone, the network of roads and trails leading to border towns and remote villages still exists. This is paradise for motorcyclists seeking to combine off-road riding with visits to colorful hill-tribe villages. The 31-mile (50-km) paved mountain road (1089) to Doi Mae Salong takes in beautiful mountain scenery and villages. Continuing out of the village, Route 1130/1338 snakes through monsoon forest, winding its way up to the 5,900-foot (1,800 m) peak of Doi Tung, where views from the summit are stunning. A short 22-mile (35-km) ride leads to Mae Sai, Thailand's northernmost town, connected to the Burmese (Myanmar) border via a road bridge over the Sai River.

After an overnight stay, head southeast riding the deserted rural roads that skirt the border with Laos. The good tarmac and lack of traffic make this region a motorcyclist's favorite. Ride the famous Doi Phu Kha Loops, adventurous mountain roads in and around the beautiful and secluded Doi Phu Kha National Park. Then follow an elevated, twisting road with fabulous views to the beautiful 13th-century Kingdom of Nan. From Nan it is about 186 miles (300 km) to Chiang Mai via rural Phayao Province. About halfway through, the city of Phayao lies beside a beautiful lake, and the ride west to Wang Nuea through magnificent forest affords great views back to it. From Chiang Mai, if you have the time, head south to Thailand's idyllic beaches. Relax under a palm and relive those heady, sweeping trails through the tropical north.

Remote villages abound in the Golden Triangle and are well worth exploring.

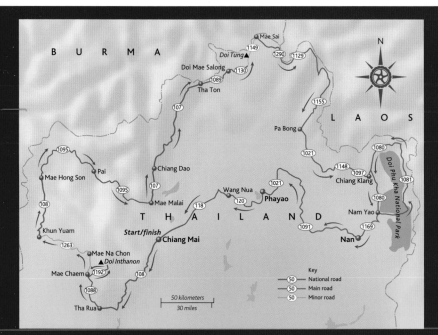

Bike: Getting your own bike into Thailand is no longer easy. However, bike hire is readily available in Chiang Mai, Chiang Rai, and Bangkok, with a good choice of brands. There are operators offering bike-inclusive tours both on- and off-road, from one day to a couple of weeks.

Weather Watch: From November to early February it is cool and dry with clear blue skies.

Extending the Ride: There is no overland connection to other featured journeys.

Ha Giang, Vietnam.

VIETNAM

A CIRCUIT NORTH FROM HANOI

Ride northwest via hill-tribe mountain villages to the hill station of Sa Pa, then north to the remote province of Ha Giang, skirting the Chinese border before returning south to Hanoi.

Ride along mountain roads through mist-shrouded valleys of lush vegetation and steamy bamboo forests. Stay in isolated villages populated by colorful mountain tribes whose culture has been preserved for centuries. The lively markets in this region attract people from their remote mountain villages to trade goods and socialize. This provides an opportunity for young men and women to meet, earning these markets the nickname "love markets." You will also have the opportunity to trek in the mountains and sample the delicious cuisine, a wonderful combination of French, Thai, and Chinese influences.

The road network is limited, with major highways often little more than a single track. This is not a full-throttle ride, but an adventure along remote roads that are rarely maintained and can throw loose gravel, potholes, and even river crossings at you. The single-track roads spiral into the mountains through stunning scenery. You do not need a big bike for this route. King of the road is the Belarusian Minsk 125cc. Affectionately known as *con trau gia* (old buffalo) by the Vietnamese, this robust little bike even has its own fan club. All mechanics know how to fix them and their spare parts are readably available, making them the ideal bikes for any trip into the mountainous north. If you prefer Japanese reliability, there is an increasing number of small capacity bikes available for hire.

The Route

The following 1,305-mile (2,100-km) circuit will take you roughly two weeks if combined with sightseeing and a few days' trekking.

above: A winding road snakes through the Ha Giang Province.

above: Riding to Dong Van in the Ha Giang Province.

far right: Big smiles on the Pha Din Pass.

Hanoi's traffic is frenetic, especially in the heat of the day when the smell of two-stroke engines fills the muggy air. Get on the road early and you will be breakfasting below purple mountains before motorcycle mayhem hits the city. NH6 is the main road northwest. It is a busy highway, so allow plenty of time for the 84-mile (135-km) ride to the Mai Chau Valley. If you prefer, take the secondary roads running parallel that lead through beautiful Muong and White Thai villages. Spend the night in the Mai Chau Valley in a stilted guesthouse, your trusty stead parked safely below with the chickens!

The next day, continue heading northwest for about 124 miles (200 km) on a road that climbs steadily, sweeping past tea and coffee plantations, through valleys, and over Chen Pass to the town of Son La, which houses the former French prison and museum. Spend the night here, rising early to visit the Black Thai morning market at Thuân Châu before riding over beautiful mountain passes including Pha Din ("Heaven and Earth"), one of the highest in the north. Stop for lunch at the town of Tuan Giáo before you tackle the rough and rocky 93-mile (150-km) road to the mountain town of Sìn Ho. The scenery is unbelievably beautiful as you traverse passes that cut though steep mountains. Stay overnight in Sìn Ho, where the market is a colorful and lively experience. The riding is easier as you leave Sìn Ho and descend into the valley, then climb over Tram Ton Pass to Sa Pa; situated at 5,249 feet (1,600 m), this popular hill resort boasts a wide range of accommodation, restaurants, and trekking options.

From Sa Pa it is about a three-hour ride along Route 70, followed by a 25-mile (40-km) dirt road to the market town of Bac Hà, frequented by the striking Flower Hmong women. From here, a further 25 miles (40 km) along a dirt road will bring you to Xín Mân. Stay to catch the Sunday market, which attracts villagers from all over the region, emerging from their remote mountain homes. Visit the market early, leaving plenty of time for the twisting, four-hour journey over mountain passes to Ha Giang, the capital of the remote northern province and the administrative center. From here it is a challenging ride that will test your skills, and your trusty Minsk, as you tackle roads that are often in very poor condition. A guide and permit is obligatory for this section, but the former will provide you with a valuable insight into the region's history and culture, taking you to villages that would otherwise prove difficult to find. You will be rewarded with incredible views from the seat of your "old buffalo" as clouds lift to reveal colorful villages hidden amongst craggy mountains and limestone pinnacles that tower above the tiny mountain roads.

The 109-mile (175-km) journey to Mèo Vac takes four hours and skirts the Chinese border through a wild, rugged landscape on roads that see very little traffic. Climb over the 4,921-foot (1,500-m) Mã Pí Lèng Pass on a road that twists up the side of an enormous canyon. Mèo Vac is lodged in a valley surrounded by vast limestone mountain ranges and perpendicular walls of rock. Spend the night in Mèo Vac to get ready for the difficult and challenging 143-mile (230-km) ride to Ba Be National Park. Your guide is invaluable for this section of the route, as you tackle forest paths, mountain passes, and river crossings. Arriving at Ba Be National Park, the sense of achievement is immense. Relax for a few days, canoe on Ho Ba Be Lake, and dine on fresh river fish.

Bike: Riding your own bike into Vietnam across the border is not an easy option. However, there are plenty of rental bikes available in Hanoi. There are operators offering bike-inclusive trips and self-guided options.

Weather Watch: The dry season runs from October to April. Avoid the rainy season during May to September when dirt roads turn to mud.

Extending the Ride: No overland connection to other featured journeys.

Remounting your Minsk, take the Colie Pass road to Cao Bang, avoiding the national highway. The 112-mile (180-km) journey is rough, but the scenery is unbelievably beautiful as you ride through dense, ancient forest. Stop for lunch in Cao Bang, then head out in the direction of Ma Phuc Pass to an area of limestone karsts and the villages of the Nùng and Tay people. Stay in one of the peaceful villages and explore the region's spectacular scenery. The Ban Gioc waterfalls form a natural border between Vietnam and China, and it is possible to take a day trip on a bamboo raft across to China on the opposite river bank.

For a scenic return to Hanoi, ride south to the border town of Tà Lùng, then over mountains and through the Dông Khê Valley to the town of Bac Son. It is a bumpy road that turns to dirt for the last 25 miles (40 km), but it winds through beautiful countryside. Stay overnight in Bac Son and return to Hanoi the next day, an easy 99-mile (160-km) ride. Wash the dirt from your trusty Minsk, its title of "old buffalo" well earned.

The Gobi Desert.

MONGOLIA

ULAANBAATAR TO GOBI DESERT LOOP

Ride a loop from Ulaanbaatar south through the Gobi Desert to a region where dinosaurs roamed and great empires flourished, returning to Ulaanbaatar via the Khogno Khan Mountains.

Imagine riding under the widest blue sky you have ever seen with only camels, sheep, and horsemen sharing the road. The sense of space and freedom as you ride across the open steppe of Mongolia is simply breathtaking. Mongolia's beauty lies in its natural wonders and hospitable people. Teenage horsemen ride like the wind, birds of prey circle the skies, and scattered across the steppe are the traditional gers (tents) of the Mongolian people. This vast land is one of the least populated countries on Earth, and the nomadic Mongolians live a life little-changed since the days of Genghis Khan, traveling by horse and living off the land. Tourist ger camps providing comfortable, traditional accommodation are scattered across the country, making it possible to experience this traditional way of life every night of your trip.

Mongolia is hard to beat when it comes to the variety of riding terrain. Ride through grassland, across desert, and over mountain passes. Potholed roads give way to stony tracks, while riding in the Gobi alternates between gray gravel and sections of deep sand. Gas stations, as we know them, do not exist, and a GPS is a welcome piece of technology in a country with so few roads. With only a handful of tarmac roads, rough tracks and horse trails connect most of this unspoiled wilderness, making it the perfect off-road motorcycling destination. If you enjoy the challenge of riding across unfamiliar terrain and spending your nights camping under a vast, star-scattered sky, then Mongolia is pure motorcycle heaven.

The Route

Allow a week to ten days for the following circular route, which provides a taste of adventurous riding across mountain, desert, and steppe.

above: Sometimes you need a helping hand.

Arrive in the capital Ulaanbaatar in early July and you will witness Mongolia's famous Naadam Festival, a three-day event that has taken place in Mongolia for centuries. Test your skills in the *eriin gurvan naadam* ("three manly games") of archery, wrestling, and horse racing. Nomads travel from some of the remotest areas of the country to celebrate the festival and show off their skills. It is a wonderful, colorful celebration of Mongolian culture with music and dancing and, of course, the Genghis Khan vodka flows into the night. Leave the festivities behind and head south into the steppe for about 155 miles (250 km) on one of the few main roads. The tarmac eventually disappears, but this is where the adventure begins as you discover for yourself the magic of this beautiful country. The final section of the day's ride is across rough dirt tracks to the spectacular granite rock formations of Baga Gazriin Chuluu, rising 5,800 feet (1,768 m) above sea level.

Relax for the evening at a nearby ger camp, rising early the next morning for the long 248-mile (400-km) ride south into the Gobi Desert to the town of Dalanzadgad. You can break the ride up at Tsagaan Suvarga, camping near these 98-foot (30-m) limestone cliffs eroded by the desert into unworldly formations. Set up at a ger camp in the region west of Dalanzadgad and explore the area, riding along stony desert tracks and testing your skills in the sandy terrain. Ride out to Bayanzag ("Flaming Cliffs"), where dinosaur eggs were discovered in the 1920s.

above: The archery competition, part of the Naadam festival.

below: A traditional Mongolian ger camp.

Visit the "glacier" canyon of Yolyn Am ("Eagle's Mouth") in the Gobi Gurvansaikhan National Park, one of Mongolia's largest national parks, extending 236 miles (380 km) from east to west and 50 miles (80 km) north to south. Gaze in awe at the immense Khongoryn Els ("Singing Sand Dunes"), Mongolia's largest dunes.

Head north again across the vast plains to the ruins of the Ongi Monastery, spending the night at a ger camp by the Ongi River. From Ongi, it is a 155-mile (250-km) ride to the Orkhon Valley and the ruined city of Karakorum, Mongolia's ancient capital. Its walls surround the exquisite Buddhist monastery of Erdene Zuu, once more an active monastery. If the riding has been a little tough, take a soak at the nearby Khujirt hot springs and relax overnight at a ger camp.

From here the 62-mile (100-km) ride northeast to the Khogno Khan Mountain Reserve takes you over rocky mountains, across steppe, and through dense forest. Spend the night at a camp close to the Mongol Els sand dunes before rejoining the tarmac for the final 186-mile (300-km) ride back to Ulaanbaatar. "The Land of Blue Skies" will leave a huge impression on you and is a truly magnificent motorcycling destination.

Bike: It is now possible to take your own bike into Mongolia. Alternatively, join an operator-run tour on their off-road bikes.

Weather Watch: July to September is really the only time to ride this route by motorcycle.

Extending the Ride: There is no overland connection to other featured journeys, but a short flight will take you to Beijing, where you can pick up a tour along the Northern Silk Road. Alternatively, pick up the Trans-Siberian Railway, which connects Mongolia with Russia and China.

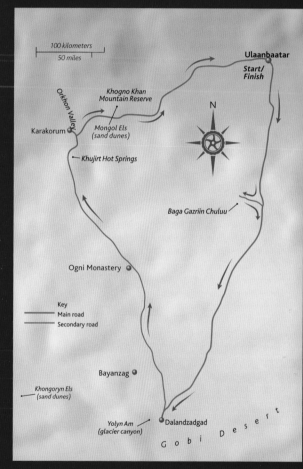

Horse racing at Naadam, another of the "three manly games."

AUSTRALASIA

Racing in the Finke Desert.

The road to Uluru.

AUSTRALIA

DARWIN TO ALICE SPRINGS: THE TOP END TO THE RED CENTRE

Ride from Darwin and the lush tropical landscape of the Top End through the arid deserts of the Northern Territory, across the Tropic of Capricorn to Australia's Red Centre.

This region of Australia is home to the Aboriginal people, and the journey starts and ends at two of their most sacred sites. Kakadu National Park in Australia's Northern Territory sits at the tip of the tropical north. The park is a breathtakingly beautiful wilderness area, and a walk among craggy escarpments reveals thousands of Aboriginal rock paintings. The lush tropical setting of the Top End is replaced by a barren, arid landscape as you ride south through the heart of the Northern Territory. Here, outback tracks branch off from the tarmac into the desert, and remote roadhouses survive on the trade of passing vehicles. As you approach the deserts of the Red Centre, strange, surreal formations appear against the vast blue skies, and the earth turns red. Here are some of Australia's most amazing natural wonders, no more so than Uluru, which rises dramatically from Aboriginal ancestral lands, changing color throughout the day and enchanting visitors from across the globe. A journey through this region gives you a momentary taste of life in the outback and a snapshot of the history of this ancient land and its people.

This is a long ride from the tip of Australia's Northern Territory to its Red Centre. The Stuart Highway, often referred to as "The Track," is named after John McDouall Stuart, the first European to cross Australia from south to north. It bisects the heart of Australia, and riding this road gives you a real appreciation for the scale of this huge country. Fully sealed in the mid-eighties, its entire length passes through remote outback Australia with services and fuel stops well signposted. You can ride for hours without seeing another vehicle along a road that stretches far into the horizon. However, this journey is not about the road. It is about the places you visit and characters you meet at the roadhouses and towns along the way, as you experience the hospitality and humor

above: Dirt roads near Alice Springs.

The Route

The Stuart Highway covers approximately 1,770 miles (2,800 km) from Darwin to Adelaide. The following route covers the 932-mile (1,500 km) section from Darwin to Alice Springs. The road can be ridden in a few days, but with visits to the national parks on either end, allow at least a week.

Leave Darwin on the Stuart Highway, but branch off east after about 28 miles (45 km) onto the Arnhem Highway for the 93-mile (150-km) ride to Kakadu National Park. It is well worth the detour for a few days to experience the incredible diversity of vegetation and animal life that thrives in the park.

Return to the highway, riding south for about 186 miles (300 km) to the town of Katherine, jumping-off point for visits to the magnificent Katherine Gorge. From Katherine it is a long, hot, and dusty 683 miles (1,100 km) to Alice Springs. The highlights of this section of the journey

top: Stopping to admire Uluru at sunset.

middle: The dusty roads of the Red Centre.

below: Darwin, where this journey begins.

are the bush pubs along the route that provide accommodation, fuel, and entertainment to passing travelers. The Larrimah Hotel, 109 miles (175 km) south of Katherine, is a typical outback pub that boasts the highest bar in the Northern Territory and the Pink Panther at the entrance. A further 62 miles (100 km) down the Track is the historic Daly Waters Pub, which has held a license since 1893. The walls are lined with visitor memorabilia, and it makes a good overnight stop to share a few beers with fellow travelers and fuel up for the approach to the deserts of central Australia.

The landscape becomes more stark and sparse as you blast down the Track for 249 miles (400 km) to Tennant Creek. There is a tale that the town was settled when a wagonload of beer broke down in the 1930s, and the drivers decided to make themselves a home while they sampled the goods. As you leave Tennant Creek, the scenery starts to transform into a rugged desert landscape. A 62-mile (100-km) ride brings you to the Devils Marbles, or Karlu Karlu—huge, rounded boulders thought by local Aborigines to be the eggs of the Rainbow Serpent. It is worth camping in the area to experience sunrise

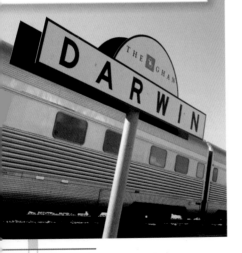

Karlu Karlu—huge, rounded boulders thought by local Aborigines to be the eggs of the Rainbow Serpent. It is worth camping in the area to experience sunrise and sunset when the Marbles and the surrounding desert landscape are truly spectacular. If you prefer a little more comfort and the chance to see an extraterrestrial, a short 16-mile (25-km) ride south brings you to Wycliffe Well, renowned for its UFO sightings and its vast range of beers. A short distance south, the Barrow Creek pub is one of the oldest roadhouses on the Track. Originally a telegraph station, it has a bloody history and is well worth a stop before the final 175-mile (282-km) push to Alice Springs.

Pass the turnoff for outback tracks that lead east to Queensland and west through the Tanami Desert before rolling into Alice Springs, "capital" of the Red Centre. It is a fun outback town surrounded by the orange and purple glow of the MacDonnell Ranges. From Alice Springs, there is a fantastic route along a combination of paved and dirt tracks out to the West MacDonnell Ranges, across to Kings Canyon via the 124-mile (200-km) Mereenie Loop, then southwest for about 199 miles (320 km) along a paved road to Uluru, which rises spectacularly from the surrounding plain.

Bike: It is possible to take your own bike into Australia. Bike hire is available in Darwin and most major cities. There are a few operators offering bike-inclusive tours.

Weather Watch: Best months for the tropical north are May to October. The Red Centre is best visited March to May and October to November.

Extending the Ride: About 249 miles (400 km) south of Alice Springs is the turnoff to the Oodnadatta Track at Marla, or continue south for 96 miles (155 km) and join the track from the mining town of Coober Pedy.

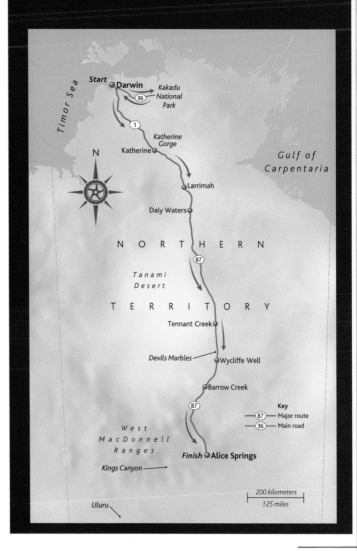

Riding the Oodnadatta Track is one of the ultimate Australian experiences.

AUSTRALIA

THE OODNADATTA TRACK

Take a ride through desert plains along the famous Oodnadatta Track in South Australia. Ride from Marree to Oodnadatta, then across to the opal-mining town of Coober Pedy.

South Australia's outback is easily accessible from Adelaide, but once out there it is hot, wild, and desolate. It's a region renowned for its larger-than-life characters, whose tall stories and humor add color to the desolate landscape. The Oodnadatta Track follows the route of the old Ghan Railway, named after the Afghan camel trails that trekked the route prior to the advent of the railway. The journey is one of discovery, the region's history unfolding along the route. End your journey in Coober Pedy, which retains the air of a frontier town, its inhabitants still mining for that perfect opal.

Ride one of Australia's legendary desert tracks. Encounter punishing corrugations, rocky tracks, and suicidal wildlife, especially around dusk. You will also encounter bulldust, a fine powder dust that can cover deep holes and look like smooth track. Once you've picked your bike up a few times, you start to spot the signs—dual sports and enduro bikes are more suited to this terrain. The condition of the track will depend on recent weather conditions; so check the weather forecast before setting out and pre-plan fuel and water stops. This is an outback track that is generally well maintained and regularly used, but don't underestimate the possible dangers. It is wild and remote, and the riding can be extremely challenging, but no trip to Australia is complete without a ride through the outback. With a little pre-planning, it will be the highlight of your visit.

The Route

Allowing for a couple of overnight stops in the outback, this route should take you three days.

above: Keep an eye out for Australia's unusual wildlife.

above: Coober Pedy, the famous opal-mining town.

far right: A welcome sight after a dusty ride.

The Oodnadatta Track begins at the old railhead of Marree. Ride out of town in the early morning light, while the air is still cool, and get onto the track. Concentration is key as you scan the road for the best line to take. If you have never ridden one of the desert pistes before, take your time while you get a feel for the terrain. About 62 miles (100 km) out of Marree, the illusion of a vast ocean shimmers on the horizon. As the mirage comes into focus, the ocean becomes the white salt crust of Lake Eyre South. Once past the salt lake, look out for a turnoff about 16 miles (25 km) further down the track. If you want to camp out under the vast outback skies, there is a campsite at Coward Springs. If you prefer a bed, William Creek lies a further 47 miles (75 km) down the Oodnadatta Track. This small town is surrounded by the world's largest cattle station. Fuel, food, camping, and accommodation are available at the famous William Creek Hotel, built in 1887 to service the Ghan Railway. Back on the track again, you'll come to the Algebuckina Railway Bridge located on the Neales River. There are waterholes here, so it is a good place to camp.

The 24-mile (200-km) ride from William Creek will take you to the town of Oodnadatta, which served as a railhead until 1929. The vision of the Pink Roadhouse is a fabulous sight after your ride through the desert. In addition to brightening up the landscape, the roadhouse provides accommodation, the legendary "Oodnaburger," and good advice about the roads ahead. The town museum gives you an insight into the lives of the local Aboriginal people and the history of the Ghan Railway. Stock up with fuel and provisions, give your bike a good check, then head back out into the desert.

The current track finishes at Marla, 124 miles (200 km) further west and out on the Stuart Highway. Alternatively, head southwest for 143 miles (230 km) across the Painted Desert to Coober Pedy, a wild opal-mining town. The road to Coober Pedy varies from wide and gravelly to stony, with plenty of hidden bulldust. The scenery on this route is awe-inspiring and the light is magical, particularly at dawn and dusk. The original *Mad Max* movies were filmed in this area, taking advantage of the vast open spaces and the lunar-like landscape. At Coober Pedy, wash off the dust at an underground hotel and join the town's residents and visitors for a well-earned beer in one of the lively bars.

Bike: It is possible to take your own bike into Australia. Bike hire is available in Melbourne and Adelaide. There are operators offering bike-inclusive tours.

Weather Watch: May to September is the best time to visit. October to March is not recommended due to high temperatures. Check conditions at www.dpti.sa.gov.au/OutbackRoads/ outback_road_conditions/area_3_oodnadatta_track.

Extending the Ride: Join the Stuart Highway at either Marla or Coober Pedy and head either north to Alice Springs or south to Adelaide.

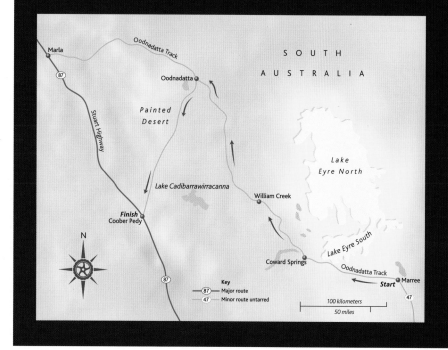

The coastal road through the Otway Range

AUSTRALIA

THE GREAT OCEAN ROAD

Ride the Great Ocean Road, which runs west along Victoria's coast for 177 miles (285 km) from Torquay to Warrnambool.

The state of Victoria lies on Australia's southwest coast. For a small state, it packs in a lot of sights, many within reach of a long day's ride out from Melbourne. Visit the spectacular rocky outcrops of the Grampians National Park, the snow-covered Victorian Alps, or the beautiful wine regions of the Yarra Valley. A highlight of any trip to this region is a ride along the Great Ocean Road. The road was blasted from the rocky cliffs along Victoria's rugged southwest coast by more than 3,000 returned soldiers in honor of their fallen comrades in WWI. It winds through rainforest and past some of the best surfing beaches in Australia, following a jagged coastline where the powerful Antarctic Ocean smashes against the rocky headlands.

This is a leisurely and scenic ride on good tarmac, giving you time to admire the outstanding views and visit places of interest along the way. The road hugs the coast between Torquay and Apollo Bay. From Apollo Bay, the road heads inland through the Great Otway National Park, rejoining the coast at Port Campbell National Park. The ride from Moonlight Head, the "Shipwreck Coast," is the most spectacular, with sandstone cliffs dropping away into the ocean and unusual rock formations rising from the ocean. The coastline can be wild and windy even during the summer months, so keep your windproof jacket on.

The Route

The Great Ocean Road could easily be ridden in a day, but take a few days to explore the wild coast, lively resort towns, and beautiful national parks that line the route.

From Melbourne, it is a 60-mile (95-km) ride southwest to Torquay and the start of the Great Ocean Road. Lively Torquay is at the center of Victoria's "surf coast," and the town buzzes during the surf season. The road continues through the town of Anglesea and onto the popular resort of Lorne. Here there is a great choice of accommodation and restaurants as well as a regular calendar of festivals throughout the year. From Lorne, the road snakes along the coastline, descending to the Wye and Kennett Rivers, tranquil spots for camping and bushwalking.

A little further along the coast, Apollo Bay nestles between green hills and wild ocean surf. Popular with artists and musicians, local pubs feature regular music sessions, and good accommodation can be found in the surrounding hills and valleys. From Apollo Bay, the Great Ocean Road heads inland through the Great Otway National Park, curving through rainforest. The final stretch from Moonlight Head is known as the Shipwreck Coast, owing to its reputation for luring victims to its rugged cliffs. For motorcyclists, this section of the road is the most fun. Views are fabulous as bends hug the coastline, offering far-reaching views of the Twelve Apostles, limestone pillars towering 213 feet (65 m) out of the ocean. Nearby Loch Ard Gorge

Otway National Park has a great treetop walk if you want a break from the bike.

was named after a ship that wrecked nearby and whose only two survivors sheltered in one of the caves. Just west of Port Campbell, the double-arched rock formation of London Bridge comes into view. The last stretch of the road winds through farming country and onto Warrnambool and the end of the Great Ocean Road.

above left: The Twelve Apostles.

above right: The Great Ocean Road runs along a beautiful stretch of coast.

Bike: It is possible to take your own bike into Australia. Bike hire is available in Melbourne. There are operators offering bike-inclusive tours.

Weather Watch: February to April is a good time to visit. The weather is warm and the beaches and towns are less crowded.

Extending the Ride: It is a further 400-mile (650-km) ride to Adelaide for routes to the Red Centre and the Oodnadatta Track.

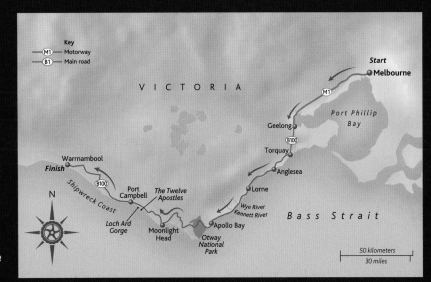

Mount Cook, the highest mountain in New Zealand.

NEW ZEALAND

SOUTH ISLAND CIRCUIT

Ride a circuit from Christchurch, encompassing much of South Island's varied landscapes and stunning roads.

New Zealand's South Island is wild and spectacular—a land of magnificent natural beauty, offering an incredible variety of vast, powerful landscapes. Awesome fjords and glaciers, rainforests, turquoise lakes, and ancient, native forests are all enclosed by a wild and rugged coastline.

New Zealand is considered one of the world's top motorcycling destinations. Perfect roads lead over hills and mountains through stunning natural wonders. Roads are generally quiet and often deserted, giving you the feeling of riding through an untouched land. Although New Zealand is a relatively small country, you will experience an incredible feeling of space, riding through a landscape that changes from farmland to alpine to tropical in just a few hours.

The Route

Allowing for sightseeing, the following loop should take roughly two weeks.

Start your trip with a ride to Aoraki/Mount Cook, New Zealand's highest peak. Head inland from Christchurch through the heart of gentle countryside. The road (SH8) rises over Burkes Pass (2,300 feet/701 m), winding to beautiful Lake Tekapo, a turquoise glacial lake framed against a backdrop of snow-capped mountain peaks. Head southwest for about 28 miles (45 km), then take the road (SH80) to Lake Pukaki for fabulous views to Mount Cook—a fantastic end to your first day's ride. From the lake, the road continues for about 37 miles (60 km) to the entrance of the Aoraki/Mount Cook National Park. If you want to explore the vast peaks and glaciers on foot, the nearby town of Twizel makes a good stopover. From Twizel, head east for about 165 miles (265 km) to the coast, following the SH1 south to Dunedin, a city with a very Scottish history. Dunedin is one of the most well-preserved Victorian and Edwardian cities in the

above: Riding near Milford Sound.

above: The Fox Glacier in the Westland National Park.

below: A woolly road block.

southern hemisphere. From here, take a ride up the Otago Peninsula for fabulous views and rugged beaches. Continue along SH1 to the Southlands region, the southeastern reaches of the island. Motorcycle legend Burt Munro was born in Invercargill, and much of the film "The World's Fastest Indian," based on his story, was shot in the area.

Leave the surf of the Pacific, riding inland toward the breathtaking wilderness of Fiordland National Park, a World Heritage Site, which includes Milford, Dusky, and Doubtful Sounds. The picturesque town of Te Anau serves as the main transport and accommodation hub, and the 75-mile (120 km) ride from here to Milford Sound is one of the most spectacular roads you will ever ride. Rise early, fill your tank with gas, and get on the road before the tourist buses. Scenery unfolds past rolling farmland as the road follows Lake Te Anau before entering verdant, dense forests. Ride past the Mirror Lakes and along the avenue of the Disappearing Mountain, which appears to shrink as you ride toward it. Climb the steep road to Homer Tunnel, a 3,999-foot (1,219-m) tunnel cut from solid rock, emerging between sheer mountain faces into Cleddau Valley. Milford Sound is an amazing 14-mile (22-km) long fjord dominated by the 5,551-foot (1,692-m) Mitre Peak. After your incredible ride, relax and appreciate the scale of this natural wonder on a scenic boat ride into the open sea.

Returning to Te Anau, a further two-and-a-half-hour scenic ride (108 miles/172 km) brings you to Queenstown, the world's adrenaline capital. If you have the urge to throw yourself out of a plane or hang from a bungee, this is undoubtedly the place to do it. Ride the 62 miles (100 km) to Wanaka over the Crown Range Road, the highest main road in New Zealand (3,688 feet/1,121 m). The narrow, paved road zigzags up the mountain, offering stupendous views down to the Arrow Valley and back to Lake Wakatipu and Queenstown. In the Cardrona Valley, look out for the infamous Bra Fence. What started as fun in the late 90s—when bras appeared on the fence—now has a more serious message. Pull over and make a "donation" in the support of the breast cancer foundation.

From Wanaka, it is a rollercoaster of a ride to the west coast over the 1,857-foot (563-m) Haast Pass, once used by the Māori in search of greenstone (jade). From Haast, a 75-mile (120-km) ride north (SH6) brings you to Westland Tai Poutini National Park. The colossal, sparkling white glaciers of Fox and Franz Josef cut through the rainforest, almost reaching the road.

Continue north (SH6) to Hokitika, which was first settled in 1860 after the discovery of gold on the west coast. Mid-March sees the town's Wildfoods Festival, where you can sample such delicacies as chocolate worm truffles and deep-fried grasshoppers. From Hokitika, the road skirts the coast, affording wonderful views. At Graymouth, head inland, returning to Christchurch over Arthur's Pass, a spectacular 143-mile (230-km) road (SH73) cutting through the breathtaking, dramatic scenery of the Southern Alps.

Bike: It is possible to take your own bike into New Zealand. Bike hire is available in Christchurch. There are operators offering bike-inclusive tours.

Weather Watch: October to May is the best time to visit. Winter runs from June to September.

Extending the Ride: No overland connection to other featured journeys.

EUROPE

Pausing on a dirt track in Iceland.

The Kjölur Route F35.

ICELAND

THE RING ROAD TOUR

From Seydisfjördur on the east coast, this route runs counterclockwise around the Ring Road (NH1), which circumnavigates the island for 832 miles (1,340 km).

Created by wild natural forces and forged from fire and ice, Iceland is a pure, wild, and untamed land of ice caps, fjords, and glaciers. Visitors are treated to volcanic eruptions, steam explosions, and bubbling mud pools. The country reshapes itself before your eyes, and as you ride around Iceland, you will witness the elements in their most raw form and nature at its most powerful.

There is no highway here, and the Ring Road, the only main paved road, has stretches of gravel, narrow passes, and blind bends, particularly in the remote and desolate northeast. If you have a dual sport bike, there are some fantastic and challenging gravel mountain roads (often referred to as highland roads) branching from the Ring Road into the wild interior. This is a country forged by the forces of nature, and the winds can be ferocious. Motorcycling here provides a real feel of experiencing the elements, not to mention the wildlife—there are more sheep in Iceland than humans, and they wander the roads at will.

The Route

A week will allow you to circuit the Ring Road and visit some of the places highlighted here, but if you allow two weeks, you will have time to get out on foot or head inland to tackle the gravel tracks and untamed interior.

From Seydisfjördur, head inland to Egilsstadir. Get onto the Ring Road, riding north through the remote wilderness of the northeast. After about 80 miles (130 km), head off the Ring Road at Grímsstadir and onto the 864, a rough gravel road that leads to the thunderous Dettifoss waterfall and Jökulsárgljúfur National Park. If you feel the need to stretch your legs after the ferry ride,

above: The Strokkur geyser erupts every five to ten minutes.

Gullfoss, one of the most popular tourist attractions in Iceland.

this is a popular area for hiking. Follow the 85 around the Tjörnes Peninsula to Húsavík. In June, beautiful purple lupines line the road as far as the eye can see. The town of Húsavík is one of the best places to go whale watching. Boats run daily from May to October, and the trips usually last about three hours. There is a good chance of seeing minke and possibly humpback and fin whales. The excellent Húsavík Whale Museum is definitely worth a visit.

Back on the Ring Road, it is worth spending a couple of days in the area around Lake Mývatn to explore the hot springs and lava towers and to walk around the crater rim of the dormant Hverfjall volcano. It is also known as "Midge Lake," so you may want to keep your visor down as you ride to keep insects from pelting your face. From Lake Mývatn, it is just over an hour's ride (62 miles/100 km) to Akureyri, Iceland's second largest town, lying just 62 miles (100 km) south of the Arctic Circle. Accommodation options are plentiful, and the town boasts the world's northernmost botanical gardens.

If you continue west along the Ring Road, the starting point to Kjölur Route F35 can be picked up just past Varmahlíd. The 125-mile (200-km) Kjölur Route F35 also cuts across the interior, providing incredible views of Langjökull and Hofsjökull glaciers. It tends to be one of the first mountain roads to open and is considered to be one of the most accessible. There are basic accommodations about halfway down the road, located close to hot springs. If you have the time, an overnight stay in the wild interior is recommended.

The Kjölur Route F35 ends in the area known as the Golden Circle, an area popular with visitors and just a short ride from Reykjavik, Iceland's vibrant capital. At Gullfoss (Golden Waterfall), torrents of water thunder into a huge gorge, and nearby you'll find the bubbling hot springs of Geysir and Strokkur,

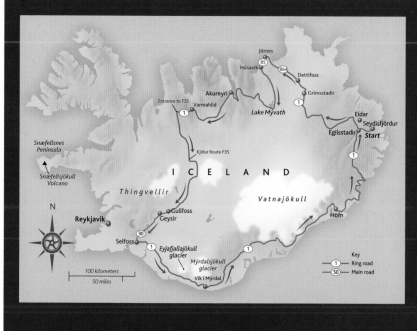

Bike: It is possible to take your own bike into Iceland. Smyril Line (*www.smyrilline.com*) runs the ferry from Denmark to Iceland. Limited bike hire is available, and there are a couple of operators offering bike-inclusive and self-guided tours.

Weather Watch: Mid-May to mid-September are the best times to ride. A June visit will give you almost 24 hours of daylight. The mountain roads are open starting in late June. The tourist board hotline provides daily road and weather information (*www.road.is*).

Extending the Ride: The Smyril ferry travels via Denmark's Faroe Islands. Some trans-Atlantic flights stop in Reykjavik, so break the flight for a week and hire a bike.

the latter of which emits jets of water and steam every few minutes. Close by is Thingvellir, the site of Iceland's democratic assemblies for more than 800 years, which perches on top of a major fault line.

Drop south back onto the Ring Road at Selfoss, heading east for 80 miles (130 km) towards Iceland's southernmost point and the black sand beaches at Vík í Mýrdal. Your ride will take you past the foot of the Eyjafjallajökull and Mýrdalsjökull glaciers; active volcanoes simmer below their icy caps. The southeast section of the Ring Road is dominated by Vatnajökull, Europe's largest ice cap. It is immense, awe-inspiring, and covers an area of 1,864 square miles (3,000 square km), its glacial fingers almost touching the road. Watch icebergs float in the deep Jökulsárlón Glacier Lagoon before leaving the south coast and climbing into the rugged alpine landscape of the eastern fjords.

From the town of Höfn, the final section of the Ring Road takes you over the Almannaskard Pass into Iceland's beautiful fjord country. Here the road winds through numerous steep-walled inlets, squeezing between mountain and sea as you make your way back to Seydisfjördur. Iceland's ride is a harsh and sometimes lonely route, yet the scenery is immensely powerful, spectacularly dramatic, and like no other place you will ever ride.

Jökulsárlón, one of a number of Iceland's glacial lakes.

The fjords of Norway are a spectacular sight.

NORWAY

FJORDLAND TO THE NORTH CAPE

This route runs through Norway's magnificent fjordland on the west coast to Nordkapp ("North Cape") in the Arctic Circle.

Leave the summer crowds behind in southern Europe and voyage north to the land of the Vikings. It is not as far away, or as cold, as you may think. The raw power and sheer magnificence of the scenery will take your breath away. The air is clear and the elements are awesome, offering rugged coastline, plunging river valleys, and those fabulous fjords.

Norway is a unique riding experience. Spectacular serpentine roads spiral skywards almost to Valhalla. Multiple switchbacks and nail-bitingly narrow roads run alongside fjords, mountains, and thundering waterfalls, cutting through rock faces and wiggling over mountains. It is often impossible to go in a straight line, with some tunnels even turning an incredible 360 degrees. Ferries are a necessity in this land of water, and the ferry journey itself is often an inexpensive means of seeing some of Norway's most impressive scenery. Almost every exhilarating road will bring a smile to your face. Best of all, the summer offers almost 24 hours of daylight—ample time to ride and ride.

The Route

The following route should take about a week, but allow yourself a little extra time if you want to explore the coast and the Lofoten and Vesterålen islands.

This route starts in Bergen, whose cobbled streets are lined with brightly painted hotels, bustling bars, and superb restaurants. Leave Bergen for the ride north on the E39 to Sognefjord, the world's longest and deepest fjord. Board the ferry and enjoy the breathtaking views of sheer cliffs and cascading waterfalls as you cross. Roll off the ferry and on to the Sognefjell Road/ Sognefjellsvegen (RV55), one of Norway's oldest trade routes running

above: Mingling with some very tame locals.

above: The Trollstigen, a rollercoaster of a road.

below: Beautiful Bergen is a lovely place to stay.

east to west between Sognefjord and the Gudbrandsdalen Valley. The road runs through the jagged peaks of the Jotunheimen Mountains to Jostedalsbreen, Norway's largest glacier, and on to the town of Lom. It is an exhilarating and breathtaking ride through lush valleys, past thunderous waterfalls, and below alpine peaks, with views of ice-blue glaciers and emerald lakes. From Lom, head 45 miles (73 km) northwest to the start of the Gamle Strynefjellsvegen Mountain Road (RV258), a 17-mile (27-km) narrow gravel road that takes you on a brief journey through true wilderness. After reaching the end of this road, head north for about 8 miles (14 km) on RV15 until you reach the Golden Route (RV63).

The Golden Route is Norway's motorcycling nirvana. Firstly, a detour on a rough mountain toll road takes you to the Dalsnibba viewpoint, affording impressive views of the Geirangerfjord where spectacular waterfalls cascade down sheer cliffs into turquoise water and mountain farms cling to the rocks. Next is the Ørnevegen ("Eagles' Highway"), a thrilling ride of multiple switchbacks. From Eidsdal, a short ferry ride connects you to the Linge Ferry Pier and the start of the Trollstigen Road. This dizzying, white-knuckled rollercoaster of a ride zigzags through eleven hairpin bends across the face of the mountain and is an engineering masterpiece. You will roll into the lovely coastal town of Åndalsnes grinning from ear to ear.

Continue onto the engineering masterpiece that is the Atlantic Road, voted Norway's "Architectural Monument of the Century." The ocean dominates this 5-mile (8-km) ride over seven bridges as the road skips across islets and skerries, linking coastal communities. Ride north from Åndalsnes on the RV64 to Molde, then on to Bud. The Atlantic Road forms part of a 22-mile (36-km) national tourist route that runs from Bud to Kårvåg, close to Kristiansund. You are now heading into the extreme environment of northern Norway.

Leaving Kristiansund, blast along the E39 to the cathedral city of Trondheim, a pleasant choice for an overnight stop. From Trondheim, it is still a long 1,013-mile (1,630-km) ride to Nordkapp through a wild and often inhospitable land. If time is short, the E6 will take you all the way, but if you have time for the longer scenic route, pick up the RV17, or Kystriksveien

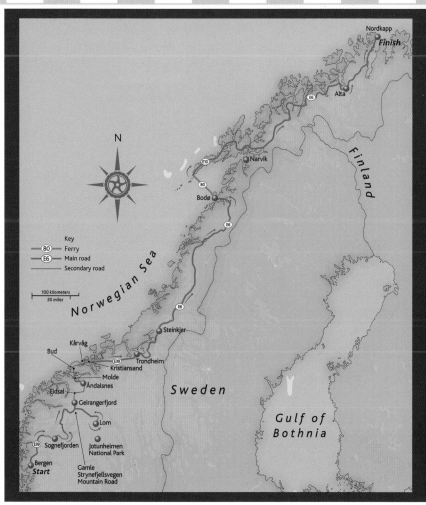

Bike: It is preferable to take your own bike into Norway, as hire options are extremely limited.

Weather Watch: Many passes are closed until June. June to August is the best time to visit, but the roads are quieter in June.

Extending the Ride: Ride into neighboring Sweden and Finland.

("coastal route"). This road follows the coast through the fishing villages of northern Norway using a network of roads, bridges, tunnels, and ferries to link the island-studded coast from Steinkjer to Bodø.

Bodø is the ferry port for the stunning Lofoten and Vesterålen islands, where colorful fishing villages perch under the peaks of the Lofotveggen ("Lofoten Wall"), a 100-mile (160-km) stretch of mountains. The islands are a picturesque and tranquil place to unwind. The E10 connects the islands to the mainland just above Narvik, where you pick up the E6 to ride through the vast Arctic wilderness of Tromsø and Finnmark, a mountain plateau of rivers and lakes with barely a tree on the horizon. It will take you about seven hours to ride to Alta, the base for travel into the interior of Finnmarksvidda. Here, the semi-nomadic indigenous Sami people, who roam the plateau living off the land and herding reindeer, populate a vast, barren mountain plateau. Get onto the E69 for the final 81-mile (130-km) push to the cliff of Nordkapp, where the Svalbard archipelago is the only dry land between you and the North Pole.

Highland roads can be wonderfully empty.

SCOTLAND

EDINBURGH TO GAIRLOCH IN THE NORTHWEST HIGHLANDS

Starting in Edinburgh, weave through Perthshire and the Great Glen to Gairloch on the northwest coast.

Once out of Edinburgh, Scotland's historic and beautiful capital, you soon find yourself riding in an unfolding landscape of soft hills and mist-shrouded glens, spectacular mountains, and a wild, rugged coast. The subtle changing light is magical as morning mists lift to reveal mountains covered in purple heather and sharp granite peaks. The light changes throughout the day, creating an atmospheric backdrop to Scotland's untamed landscape.

Scotland feels wonderfully remote, yet distances across some of the best biking roads in Europe are often quite short. Single-track roads twist across mountains, skirt around lochs, and weave through glens. It takes only minutes to slip away from the crowds onto deserted roads that lead across moors and to the craggy coastline and rocky beaches. For riders in search of solitude and days of long, empty roads, Scotland is hard to beat.

The Route

This route can easily be ridden in a few days, but allow at least a week if you wish to combine your riding with sightseeing and relaxing on the northwest coast.

An hour and a half's ride north of Edinburgh (A823) through Perthshire's soft glens and magnificent woodland brings you to Crieff, a genteel spa town and home of Glenturret, one of Scotland's oldest distilleries. From Crieff, head west for a further 30 minutes to the village of Tyndrum, where you can refuel both yourself and the bike and use the helmet wash provided by the biker-friendly Green Welly Stop. It is a wild 31-mile (50-km) ride (A82) across Rannoch Moor on a fabulous motorcycle road with long, sweeping bends and a good, grippy surface. The road snakes across dramatic, desolate moorland to arrive at beautiful Glencoe, a magnificent, moody

above: Eilean Donan Castle.

below: Catching the evening sun.

mountain valley with a glorious and bloody history. Stay a few days and soak up the atmosphere while walking among the mountains.

Leave Glencoe, blasting north for about half an hour to Fort William. You are now deep into Highland territory and the Great Glen, which is a wall of mountains and lochs that cuts across the Highlands from Fort William north to Inverness. Look out for the Commando Monument just north of Spean Bridge, then slip off the main road at Invergarry just 25 miles (40 km) north of Fort William. Take an hour's ride west (A87) on a good, fast road that climbs high through forest, opening out to reveal magnificent views down to Loch Cluanie before snaking through the mountains of Glen Shiel. You'll pass the awesome Five Sisters of Kintail to one of Scotland's famous landmarks, Eilean Donan Castle. From here, head north for 41 miles (65 km) (A890), winding your way around Lochcarron onto the Applecross Peninsula and the infamous Bealach na Ba—the "Pass of the Cattle"—for an exhilarating ride of hair-raising switchbacks across bleak moorland. Challenging bends take you to the summit of the highest road in the highlands, ascending 2,050 feet (625 m) in just 6 miles (10 km); the views from the top are superb.

Stay overnight in the village of Applecross, then ride north along the narrow single-track road that hugs the coast around the peninsula. The views are fabulous and an early start means you are likely to have this spectacular road all to yourself as you weave your way to Loch Torridon, the northern boundary of the peninsula. Just 8 miles (12 km) north of Torridon lay the beautiful pine-covered islands of Loch Maree. The dramatic and imposing landscape that surrounds the loch unfolds as you skirt the shores on the A832,

Glencoe has beautiful views and a bloody history.

Bike: It is possible to take your own bike into Scotland. Bike hire is available in Glasgow and Edinburgh. There are operators offering bike-inclusive tours.

Weather Watch: April to September is the best time to visit.

Extending the Ride: Cross the border into Northern England. Take a boat from Stranraer near Glasgow to Belfast in Northern Ireland. Boats from Rosyth near Edinburgh will get you into Europe.

which then cuts inland and across to the coast. The village of Gairloch is situated around the shores of a beautiful sea loch, looking west across to the Skye and the Outer Hebrides. Ride out to long, sandy beaches set against a backdrop of the ancient Torridon Mountains, take a boat trip out to see abundant wildlife, or replace your bike boots with hiking boots and head up wonderful mountain paths. Gairloch has a wealth of accommodations and activities and makes a perfect base to explore the wild, beautiful coastline of Scotland's northwest.

far right: Gairloch, in the far northwest of Scotland.

The cliffs of Moher.

IRELAND

CORK TO THE CLIFFS OF MOHER

**From the lively city of Cork, this route takes you southwest
to the three peninsulas, then north to the dramatic Cliffs of Moher.**

The southwest corner of the Emerald Isle is a magical land of soft green hills and misty lakes. The spectacular craggy coast rises from the Atlantic, dropping to deserted beaches and encircling wild mountains. Welcoming pubs ring with infectious Irish humor and traditional live music, and if you time it right, there are traditional festivals throughout the summer.

Follow scenic roads that snake along the shoreline of the three peninsulas: wild, remote Beara; Iveragh, with its famous Ring of Kerry; and the stunning Dingle Peninsula. Ride over scenic passes for breathtaking views, pull over at tranquil beaches, or join in the *craic* (lively socializing) at lively towns and villages. This is an unhurried ride through a peaceful landscape on paved roads that are often empty, and sometimes a little bumpy, but contoured to the rolling hills they traverse.

The Route

Daily distances are short, so a week will allow time for a leisurely ride and at least one night on each of the three peninsulas.

The city of Cork is a major port and, as with most port cities, it benefits from a lively nightlife with plenty of live music playing at the pubs. Blarney Castle, with its famous stone, sits just northwest of the city, so kiss the stone and gain the gift of the gab to make ready for your ride in the Emerald Isle. As you head west from Cork to the Beara Peninsula, the forested green countryside soon gives way to a wild, windswept landscape that at times feels almost alpine. If you want to stay on the peninsula, try the popular village of Glengarriff, about 50 miles (80 km) from Cork. Traffic is light and you will have the roads to yourself as you head toward the tip of the peninsula. The highlight of any ride

above: One of Dingle's lively bars.

The Dingle Peninsula.

through the Beara Peninsula is the Healy Pass, a narrow mountain road that cuts through the heart of the Caha Mountains, affording breathtaking views from the summit. From the head of the Beara Peninsula, detour north (R569 & N22) to Killarney, a popular tourist town that plays host to Ireland BikeFest in June. Join in the fun, sample the Guinness, and pick up some tips from local riders before you ride the Ring of Kerry, the scenic 109-mile (175-km) road that encircles the Iveragh Peninsula. It is possibly Ireland's most famous road, and therefore very popular. The road meanders past mountains and lakes and through picturesque villages. Ride from Killarney through the Killarney National Park toward Moll's Gap. Ride through the pretty village of Sneem and on to Caherdaniel on the southern point of the peninsula. The road climbs steeply up and over the Coomakista Pass, affording superb views. Below the pass lies Derrynane Bay, a pleasant area to stay if you want to avoid the crowds. Cahersiveen, on the northern rim, sits at the foot of Bentee Mountain and is one of the westernmost towns in Europe.

As you ride across the northern rim of the peninsula, there are great views across to Dingle Bay, your next destination. When you reach the town of Killorglin, look out for the statue of a goat perched on a boulder. Every year, around the beginning of August, a wild mountain goat is crowned King Puck, and celebrations last for several days. Puck Fair is Ireland's oldest festival, with official records dating back to the early 17th century, although it is thought to have much older pagan origins.

The Dingle Peninsula is sprinkled with archaeological sites and long, sandy beaches. It is a predominantly Gaelic-speaking area, so road signs can get interesting. A direct narrow 6-mile (10-km) road will take you from the Ring of Kerry across to Castlemaine on the peninsula's southern rim. Enjoy riding the long, straight road along the southern edge (R561), which passes the long sandy beach at Inch and the famous South Pole Inn at the village of Annascaul. Dingle Town makes a great base, with its beautiful harbor, places to stay, and pubs that reverberate with traditional music.

Ride the stunning circuit around the tip of the peninsula along Slea Head. Return to Dingle Town to cross the steep, narrow Conor Pass, which cuts across a ridge of mountains to the north coast, ascending over 1,640 feet (500 m) for fabulous views. Once over the Conor Pass, ride east (R560 and N86) to Tralee at the head of the peninsula, then about 31 miles (50 km) north (N69) to Tarbert. Catch the car ferry across the River Shannon to Killimer. Pick up the coastal road (N67) for about an hour to the mighty Cliffs of Moher, which rise 700 feet (213 m) out of the Atlantic Ocean. The dramatic wave-battered coastline is an awesome sight. Roll up for sunset and watch the sun's dying rays warm up the rocks before dipping below the Atlantic.

Key

N22	National Primary road
N69	National secondary road
R56	Regional road

Bike: It is possible to take your own bike into Ireland. Due to prohibitive insurance costs, bike hire is very limited. Depending on your route, it is sometimes easier to hire in Northern Ireland. There are operators offering tours.

Weather Watch: May to September is the best time to visit.

Extending the Ride: Catch a ferry from Dublin to England's northwest coast, or from Belfast to Stranraer, near Glasgow.

The Ring of Kerry.

Whitby, with its famous abbey visible at the top of the hill.

ENGLAND

KENDAL TO WHITBY

From Kendal in the English Lake District, ride through the Yorkshire Dales and the North York Moors to Whitby on the east coast.

North Yorkshire is one of the few places in England where you really can escape to a wild, wide land of heather-clad moors, limestone scars, and pure, clean air. The untamed beauty and solitude of the moors will take your breath away, while ancient abbeys and formidable castles mark the landscape—yet drop down to the dales and you enter a soft countryside of historic market towns and pretty villages filled with blossom, where the local pubs serve real Yorkshire helpings and the tea shop rules supreme.

The roads in North Yorkshire are superb and offer some of the best biking in England, twisting and sweeping through sunny dales and across wild moors. The tarmac is generally good and views from the saddle are fabulous. Motorcycling is big in North Yorkshire, and biker-friendly cafés and pubs line the favorite routes. The roads really are a biking nirvana and can resemble a racetrack on a sunny Sunday, but take to the road mid-week or on a cool evening and you will have them all to yourself.

The Route

This journey features just a taste of the superb riding and stunning scenery you can expect from a ride in North Yorkshire. The following route can be ridden in a day, but two days will allow time for sightseeing and an overnight stay in the Dales.

From Kendal in the Lake District, the A684 runs east into the Yorkshire Dales. It is a very popular motorcycling road, combining hairpins, sweeping bends, and reasonably fast straights on good, smooth tarmac. The first 27 miles (44 km) to the popular market town of Hawes take you over the dramatic

above: Picturesque villages dot this route.

Perfect English motorcycling.

scenery of Garsdale Head and Mossdale Moor. The name, Hawes, means a "pass between mountains," and it stands between Buttertubs and Fleet Moss. The town makes a good base for touring Wensleydale and the adjoining dales of Swaledale, Cotterdale, Dentdale, Garsdale, Wharfedale, and Chapel-le-Dale. It is also home to Wensleydale Cheese (yes, cheese, Gromit!) and the Dales Countryside Museum.

From Hawes, continue for 16 more miles (26 km) on the A684 to Leyburn, stopping en route at Aysgarth Falls, where the River Ure tumbles over a series of broad limestone steps. Alternatively, take the high single-track road that loops through the rugged heart of Swaledale, providing far-reaching views as you ride for around 31 miles (50 km) north over the Buttertubs to the village of Thwaite, then east to the village of Reeth and high over wild Redmire

Moor. The imposing walls of 14th-century Bolton Castle loom into view as
you drop down off the moor to rejoin the A684 as it leads into the market
town of Leyburn, another great center from which to base yourself for a few
days. There is an abundance of accommodation and eateries in the town and
surrounding villages.

From Leyburn, head to Masham on the A6108, a short ride of around 11
miles (18 km). The landscape is softer as the road winds past Jervaulx Abbey
and through the lovely town of Middleham, famous for its medieval castle (once
home to Richard II) and its racing stables. The town square in Masham is a
popular pull-in for bikers and the home of the Theakstons and Black Sheep
breweries. Return to the fast straights and sweeping bends of the A6108 as it
continues through the lovely village of West Tanfield on the River Ure to the

tiny cathedral city of Ripon. If you are in the area overnight, head to the obelisk in Ripon's market square at nine o'clock for the nightly horn-blowing ceremony, which dates back possibly as far the 12th century.

Spend the evening in the Ripon area and start the following day with a big Yorkshire breakfast to set you up for your ride through the North York Moors to the North Sea coast. From Ripon, a 20-minute ride east (A61) takes you to the traditional market town of Thirsk, ideally positioned midway between the beautiful Yorkshire Dales and the dramatic North York Moors. Thirsk is famous for its racecourse and as the home of James Herriot, whose books about his life as a country vet were turned into a popular TV series. His house and surgery

Riding across heather-clad moors.

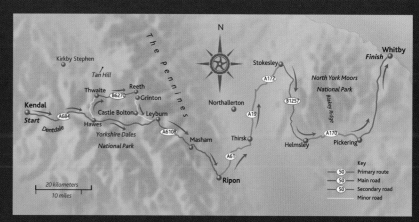

have been converted into a museum. Thirsk's other famous son, Thomas Lord, the founder of Lord's Cricket ground, was born here in 1755; his birthplace is now Thirsk Museum.

From Thirsk, take a short ride northeast (A19/A172) for around 20 miles (32 km) to Stokesley for the start of the "Helmsley TT," a superb 20-mile (32-km) run through the valleys and woodland of the Cleveland Hills to the town of Helmsley, another very popular biker meeting point. The annual MAG (Motorcycle Action Group) Farmyard Party held nearby is not to be missed if you are passing through in August. From Helmsley, it is a great hour's ride (33 miles/54 km) (A170/A169) over the heather-clad North York Moors to Whitby. About halfway along the A169, pull over at Saltergate for the dramatic panorama over the Hole of Horcum. The hollow is 400 feet (122m) deep and stretches approximately three quarters of a mile (1.2 km) across. Roll into the picturesque east coast town of Whitby, famous for its connections with Captain Cook and Bram Stoker's *Dracula*. The cliff-top abbey dominates the town, and views from the coastal path are superb. Whitby's other claim to fame is its fresh fish, so park and wander along the pier with some delicious fish and chips.

One of Yorkshire's many tea shops.

The scenic roads of the Mosel Valley.

GERMANY

RHINELAND WINE TRAILS AND THE NÜRBURGRING

This route follows Germany's Rhine river, then heads northwest to The Nürburgring.

Combine a leisurely ride along the Rhine with the thrill of riding the longest and possibly the most demanding circuit in the world. The Ring is a legend and a piece of racing history. Opened in 1927, the circuit was designed as the ultimate challenge to test the world's best riders and drivers. The Nürburgring, or Nordschleife, is also one of the most beautiful circuits, winding its way through lovely Rhineland countryside. Imagine the combined joy of riding on a long mountain road that is also a racetrack, perfect ingredients to get the heart pumping. If you've always wanted to experience the adrenaline rush of riding a race circuit, this is the opportunity of a lifetime.

The Nürburgring lies 56 miles (90 km) southwest of Cologne in the mountainous Eifel region of the Rhineland, a superb region for motorcycling. Sweeping, well-surfaced roads cut through a landscape of rolling hills, valleys lined with vineyards, crater lakes, and extensive wooded slopes. There are bike-friendly hotels along the way and close to the Ring, providing lockable parking, drying rooms, and often repair services. If you are traveling alone, it is a great way to meet fellow motorcyclists, as you can be sure someone will be heading to the Ring.

The Route

Combine a ride around the Nürburgring with a few days touring the Rhineland.

The 800-mile (1,300-km) long Rhine is one of Europe's historic rivers and has been a wine-producing region since the Romans introduced grape cultivation to the Rhine valley. Start your ride in the region of Rheingau, in southwest Germany, and by the section of the mighty Rhine known as the Romantic

above: Riding the German Wine Route.

above: Boppard am Rhein.

below: Cochem Imperial Castle, in the Mosel Valley.

Rhine. This is where the river carves through slate mountains, weaving its way below vine-covered hills and the numerous castles of the medieval robber barons who extorted tolls on merchants trading along the Rhine. From the town of Rüdesheim, the scenic B42 winds along the eastern banks of the Rhine towards Koblenz. Castles and fortresses dominate cobblestone villages and beautifully preserved historic towns surrounded by vine-clad slopes and forested hills. Car ferries cross the river at a number of places, so take a scenic and leisurely ride through one of Germany's most important wine growing areas. Follow the Rhine to the pretty town of Boppard on the western side of the river, a good overnight option if you want to spend time in the area. From Boppard, the Rhine snakes towards the city of Koblenz, the setting for a magnificent firework display at the Rhein in Flammen (Rhine in Flames) festival in August. This is where the Rhine meets the river Mosel, flowing east from France. The Mosel is another of Germany's lovely wine routes, so if you have enjoyed riding the Rhine, allow a few days to explore the Mosel Weinstrasse, also known as the Roman Wine Road. It weaves its way to the city of Trier, once the capital of the Western Roman Empire.

From Koblenz it is a short 37-mile (60-km) ride northwest to the Nürburgring, just enough time to warm up the tires. The Ring was originally built as a combined test track and race circuit. When not in use, it is available for public use. It is officially a one-way public toll road, and German road rules apply on the track. You can ride any type of motorcycle, but it must be road legal. There is no speed limit, but there is a noise limit of 95 decibels. Tickets are available on site, and the seriously obsessed can even obtain an annual ticket. You turn up, pay your money, and ride the lap of a lifetime. There are 13 miles (21 km) of track with 73 bends—that's 33 left- and 40 right-handers, so don't forget your knee-sliders. The Ring is no modern race circuit, but a series of blind bends, steep inclinations, and constantly changing road surfaces. This is an unforgiving and demanding circuit, so be realistic about your riding capabilities. There are training schemes aimed at teaching you the perfect techniques for taking to the track with confidence and making the most of this amazing circuit. It isn't a race, and there is no champagne at the end unless you bring your own. It is just the incredible opportunity to ride in the tracks of some of the world's best riders and drivers. Relax and enjoy the experience of riding one of motor racing's legendary circuits.

Bike: It is possible to take your own bike into Germany. Bike hire is available in most major cities. There are operators offering bike-inclusive tours and hotels that offer guided routes.

Weather Watch: See *www.nuerburgring.de* for opening dates and track experiences.

Extending the Ride: Head across to Zurich for a ride around the Alps, or head into France.

The Nürburgring.

Riding in the French Alps.

FRANCE

ANNECY CIRCUIT VIA THE CÔTE D'AZUR

From Annecy in the Rhône-Alpes, ride south to pick up the historic Route Napoléon through Provence to the Côte d'Azur, returning to Annecy over high alpine passes that form sections of La Route des Grande Alpes, possibly one of Europe's best-known motorcycle touring routes.

The diversity of the landscape in the southeast corner of France will surprise anyone visiting for the first time. It boasts mighty alpine peaks and high-altitude passes that stretch as far as the chic resorts of the Côte d'Azur on the Mediterranean coast, while rural Provence is covered with lavender fields and lovely hilltop towns and villages. Wherever you ride and whatever your budget, the fabulous food and wine will be an additional highlight of any visit to the region.

France is a firm favorite with European motorcyclists due to racetrack-smooth roads that fly through a constantly changing landscape. The toll roads are fast and generally in excellent condition, while high passes twist over the Alps in a series of tight hairpins, swooping down to beautiful valleys. The temptation to be throttle-happy is high, but be warned: speeding fines are on the spot and the gendarmes will happily fine you if caught.

The Route

The following route can be ridden in two to three days. Alternatively, allow a few extra days and flavor the fantastic riding with overnight stays in the mountains and rural Provence.

The beautiful town of Annecy lies on the shores of the Lac d'Annecy. Surrounded by mountains, its stunning location, set within the French Alps and close to the Swiss and Italian Alps, make it a perfect base for exploring the region. The town and surrounding villages merit a visit of at least a few days. It is also a great starting point for the 65-mile (105-km) ride south to Grenoble and the historic Route Napoléon, which follows the route taken by Napoléon Bonaparte in 1815, following his exile on Elba.

above: Cime de la Bonette.

Considered by many to be one of the best bike roads in Europe, the N85 starts in the mountains and passes through dramatic scenery as it sweeps south to the Mediterranean via Digne-les-Bains, Sisteron, and Castellane, gateway to the magnificent Gorges du Verdon (Europe's largest canyon). The N85 is an excellent, fast road that is perfect for sports bikes. The tarmac is superb, and the corners a sublime combination of seriously fast sweepers and mountain hairpins. You are guaranteed to grin all the way. At just over 186 miles (300 km) from Grenoble to Cannes on the Côte d'Azur, you will have time to lunch at one of Provence's pretty hilltop villages and then spend the early evening cruising the Riviera, or chasing sports cars along the three corniche roads that run through the heart of the French Riviera.

above: The glamorous Côte d'Azur.

below: Annecy, a beautiful town in the south of France.

Spend the night in Nice and leave early, riding north into the rugged peaks and valleys of the Mercantour National Park, a little-known region that offers peace and tranquility after the hedonistic pleasures of the Côte d'Azur. This is where the landscape changes from Mediterranean to Alpine, and at its heart the cobbled streets of Saint-Martin-Vésubie provide accommodation, food, and wine. From here it is a two-hour (68 mile/110 km) ride through the Tinée Valley to Barcelonnette (D2205) over the Cime de la Bonette (9,186 feet/2,800 m), a road that climbs almost into the clouds as it snakes past silent peaks, the clouds occasionally parting to offer magical views. Enjoy lunch at Barcelonnette's pretty café-lined square, then head north (D902) via the tight hairpins and steep ascents and descents of some of the most famous peaks of La Route des Grande Alpes.

Encounter the wild beauty of the Col de Vars, then tackle the barren slopes and switchbacks of the Col d'Izoard. Take a break and admire the incredible views in the fortified old mountain town of Briançon, one of the highest towns in Europe. This picturesque town offers food and accommodation if you want to overnight in the mountains before hitting the road again on the Col du Lautaret and Col du Galibier. Next up is the mighty Col d'Iseran. When it was officially opened in 1937, it was the highest road pass in Europe and is still considered one of the major "must ride" passes in the Alps. From the lively town of Bourg-Saint-Maurice, host to a number of summer events, go over the Cormet de Roselend and down to the pretty town of Beaufort for the final 37 miles (60 km) to Annecy, where you can enjoy a well-earned candlelit supper by the side of the lake.

Bike: It is possible to take your own bike into France. Bike hire is available throughout France. There are operators offering bike-inclusive tours.

Weather Watch: June to September is the best time to visit. Some of the higher passes are closed until well into June. Traffic is at its heaviest from late July to late August.

Extending the Ride: It is a short ride to the Swiss and Italian Alps. Alternatively, head southwest to the Pyrenees.

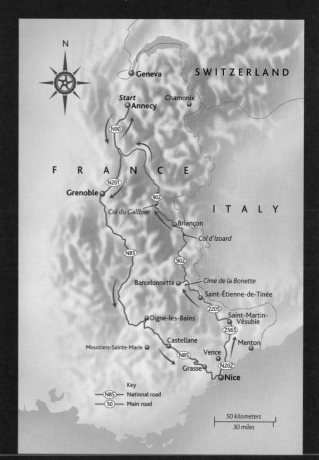

Winding through the Pyrenees.

SPAIN/FRANCE

BILBAO TO PERPIGNAN LOOP

Stretching from the Spanish Atlantic coastline to the French Mediterranean and back, this route takes in the best of the mountain roads on both sides of the Pyrenees, the tiny principality of Andorra, and a healthy slice of Catalonia.

Forming a stunning natural border between France and Spain, the Pyrenees are a motorcyclist's dream. Switchbacks and hairpins sweep over the mountains that divide the two countries and, at just over 248 miles (400 km) long and 31 miles (50 km) broad at the widest point, it is possible to breakfast on coffee and croissants in France, have tapas for lunch in Spain, and return to France to dine on the *plat du jour* washed down with locally produced wine. The Principality of Andorra, wedged between the two, is completely encircled by snow-topped mountains. Added to the fantastic riding is the change in landscape, climate, and culture as you ride from the Atlantic to the Mediterranean, or cross the border using the numerous mountain passes.

Motorcyclists are spoiled for choice—the roads are fantastic in whichever direction you ride. Go to Barcelona in June for the MotoGP, replace those leathers with some tax-free shopping in Andorra, and top it all by riding some of the most superb motorcycling roads in Europe. Road surfaces are generally excellent and often traffic-free, especially in Spain. Snow-topped peaks, limestone pinnacles, and medieval castles tower over roads that lead to glaciers, lakes, and secluded valleys. There are sweeping bends, hairpins, long fast straights, corkscrew loops, uphill climbs, and tricky, twisty turns that ensure your knee-sliders will work overtime!

The Route

This route will give you a flavor of both the French and Spanish sides of the Pyrenees and should take roughly two weeks, allowing time to combine your riding with some sightseeing.

above: Playa del Sardinero, San Sebastián.

Riding with friends in the Pyrenees.

Rolling off the boat at Bilbao, you are riding straight into Green Spain. If you prefer to take it easy on your first day while you find your land legs, a quick 63-mile (100-km) blast gets you to San Sebastián a little further along the coast. This is a town famous throughout Spain for its cuisine. Spend a lazy afternoon on the beach, then treat yourself to a celebratory meal of *pintxos* (Basque tapas) at one of the great restaurants in the old town.

The next day, get an early start on the N240/A-1 heading toward the town of Jaca. It is a good road with great views and can easily be ridden in a day whether you start from Bilbao or San Sebastián. The lakeside section between Yesa and Puente la Reina de Jaca is particularly lovely. There are some stunning roads in the area that snake through valleys to beautiful secluded villages. The Valle de Hecho and Valle de Ansó lie just northwest of Jaca, and there is now a road connecting the two. Jaca is a fairly large and lively town, and it makes a good base from which to explore the western Pyrenees.

At Jaca, you join the legendary N260. This is the ultimate biking road. Well-surfaced, it wiggles all the way to the Mediterranean coast and up to the French border. A five-hour ride on this fabulous road brings you to the lovely cathedral city of La Seu d'Urgell with its historic quarter of arcaded streets and old mansions. From here, head north into Andorra, stop for coffee, do some shopping, and stay the night before dropping back into Spain at Bourg-Madame. From here, get on to the Collada de Toses (N152/N260). This is a 28-mile (40-km) joyride of fast bends on perfect tarmac and a favorite with locals. Meet other riders at the midway car park, swap route notes, and race into Ripoll with its famous Benedictine monastery. If you've timed your ride to coincide with the annual MotoGP in June, cut south from Ripoll to the racetrack just outside Barcelona. It is a reasonably fast 65 miles (104 km) and should take just a couple of hours. Join thousands of fans at one of the world's most atmospheric and fun race days. The enthusiasm of the Spanish fans has to be experienced—they are truly crazy about their motorcycle racing and stage a fantastic event. Barcelona itself is a classic European city packed with sights and culture worthy of a detour.

From Barcelona, head north back to the Pyrenees, or continue from Ripoll along the N260. Either way you will ride through Figueres, Salvador Dalí's hometown and the location of the Teatre-Museu Dalí, a must if you have any interest in surrealist art. From here, follow the N260 north as it twists along the rugged Catalan coast, merging into the N114 as you cross the border into France and the popular town of Perpignan. The riding on either side of the eastern

Bike: It is possible to take your own bike into France and Spain. Bike hire is available in major French and Spanish cities, including Bilbao. There are operators offering bike-inclusive tours.

Weather Watch: Daytime temperatures are pleasant April to May and mid-to-late September. June to August is hot and the crowds increase.

Extending the Ride: Continue your riding in France by heading southeast to experience the Route Napoléon or La Route des Grandes Alpes, or from Bilbao head into Green Spain or south to Andalucía.

Pyrenees is a motorcycling playground, so unpack for a few days and play on the passes. Biker-run hotels in charming villages perched high in the hills make a great base for you to sample locally produced food and wine and meet other riders.

From Perpignan, head west on the D117 and you cannot go wrong. This region is famous for its Cathar castles, and the impressive Château de Peyrepertuse is just 31 miles (50 km) north. At Quillan, head southeast on the D613 over the Col du Chioula to the mountain resort of Ax-les-Thermes. Then, pick up the N20 to the small town of Tarascon-sur-Ariège, a center for visiting the prehistoric cave art in the area. From Tarascon-sur-Ariège, take the D618 over the Col de Port (4,100 feet/1,250 m) to the town of Saint-Girons.

Next up is the 3,507-foot (1,069-m) Col de Portet d'Aspet, followed closely by the Col des Ares (2,614 feet/797 m). Pick up the D125 to Bagnères-de-Lucon, returning to the D618 for a thrilling ride over the 5,147-foot (1,569-m) Col de Peyresourde, then over the 4,885-foot (1,489-m) Col d'Aspin. To complete the circuit, make your way northwest to Lourdes, famous for the apparitions of the Virgin Mary by Bernadette Soubirous in the 19th century. From Lourdes it is a short 25-mile (40-km) ride to the city of Pau, returning via Biarritz on the wild Atlantic coast to the port at Bilbao. This is a region that, once discovered, you will return to time and again, finding new riding routes each visit.

Park and admire the views.

Good weather is almost guaranteed in Spain.

SPAIN

A CIRCUIT OF ANDALUCÍA

Starting in Málaga, this route takes in the Sierra Nevada Mountains and the Cazorla Natural Park; the Moorish cities of Granada, Córdoba, and Seville; and the wild Costa de la Luz, returning to Málaga via the Sierra de Grazalema.

This is the land of fiestas and fun-loving people. The riding is relaxed and the sun always seems to shine. Spend your days circling the switchbacks of the sierras and exploring the unique Moorish architecture, and your evenings enjoying the party atmosphere of Andalucía's towns and villages.

The Spanish are passionate about bikes, ensuring a warm welcome to visiting motorcyclists. Roads are well paved with plenty of curves and twists in the mountain ranges. The whole region is crisscrossed by off-road trails, so if you've never ridden off-road but would like to try, then Andalucía is a great place to learn. Add to this the long sandy beaches, historic cities, and great food and wine, and you have a winning blend. For a vacation combined with great riding, Andalucía is hard to beat.

The Route

The following route gives you a taste of Moorish Spain and the roads of the high Sierras. It can be ridden in a week, but allow longer if you wish to combine riding with sightseeing, relaxing on the beach, or exploring the national parks.

From Málaga, it is about a 62-mile (100-km) ride east to the twisty mountain roads of the Sierra Nevada and the valleys of Las Alpujarras. Ride over beautiful mountain passes and enjoy panoramic views. When you have finished playing on the superb roads, drop down from the mountains to the Moorish city of Granada. The city's jewel is the magnificent Alhambra palace, framed against a backdrop of the Sierra Nevada Mountains. Granada is a beautiful city, so stay a few days before

above: The Jerez Moto GP attracts large crowds.

above: The city of Ronda, in the Spanish province of Málaga.

below: The magnificent Alhambra palace in Granada.

heading northeast for about 125 miles (200 km) to the Cazorla Natural Park for spectacular scenic riding on paved and dirt roads.

From Cazorla, take a ride over the 4,000-foot (1,200-m) Puerto de las Palomas ("mountain pass of the doves") and down to Empalme del Valle, where it turns north to follow the Guadalquivir Valley. Pick up the N322 for about two hours to Córdoba, where you can lose yourself in the labyrinthine old quarter surrounding the 8th-century Mezquita—a building that has been both church and mosque over the centuries—and the medieval Alcázar de los Reyes Cristianos with its magical gardens.

Take the scenic A431, which follows the Río Guadalquivir for about 81 miles (130 km) to Seville, Andalucía's capital city, then climb to the top of the La Giralda Minaret for far-reaching views. Moorish influence is strong here in the city's food and culture. Bars and restaurants line the medieval cobbled streets of the Barrio Santa Cruz, and as the sun sets, the sound of live music and flamenco dancing entices visitors to party with the locals until dawn.

From Seville, head an hour south to the lovely town of Jerez de la Frontera. In May, the race circuit here attracts thousands of spectators from all over Europe for the Jerez MotoGP. If you need proof that the Spanish love motorcycling, just join the crowds and get caught up in the excitement.

From Jerez, ride southeast (N340) along the Costa de la Luz—the wild, unspoiled face of Andalucía with its white, sandy beaches and jagged cliffs. High winds and surging ocean waves provide a constant cool breeze—a welcome relief if you have been riding in Andalucía's hot, dry center. If you love seafood, head to the natural harbor of Cádiz, where its 18th-century plazas are filled with cafés and bars serving the day's catch.

From Cádiz, it is just over 62 miles (100 km) south toward the town of Tarifa on Andalucía's southern tip, where you can rest for the night. From Tarifa, take a ride north to Ronda, which sits astride the El Tajo Gorge and amongst the Serrania de Ronda Mountains. The scenic route (A369) takes you through the Los Alcornocales Natural Park and into the Sierra de Grazalema Natural Park on a road that twists and turns as it climbs, and then drops to long, sweeping bends. The views are spectacular and the landscape constantly changing as rugged limestone cliffs, gullies, and gorges replace cork forests. In spring, mimosa and almond blossoms sweeten the air as the road sweeps toward the town of Ronda, a popular pull-in for motorcyclists. Drop into town for spectacular views of the gorge before joining yet another scenic, sweeping road east (A366), taking you 62 miles (100 km) back to Málaga and the Mediterranean coast.

Despite winding hairpin roads, the riding is relaxed here.

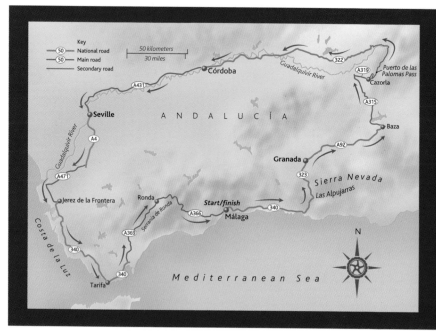

Bike: It is possible to take your own bike into Spain. Málaga and Seville offer a wide choice of bike hire. There are operators offering bike-inclusive tours both on- and off-road.

Weather Watch: March to May and mid- to late September offer pleasant daytime temperatures. Avoid June to August when it is crowded and very hot.

Extending the Ride: Take the ferry to Morocco from Tarifa or Algeciras. Alternatively, head north into the Pyrenees.

Stunning Alpine scenery.

SWITZERLAND/ AUSTRIA

THE SWISS ALPS TO THE AUSTRIAN TYROL

Start in Switzerland, dip briefly into Italy, and then ride up into the Austrian Tyrol.

The Alps stretch from Austria and Slovenia in the east, through Switzerland, Liechtenstein, Italy, and Germany to France in the west. The region boasts a pristine beauty, crisp mountain air, and some of the most gorgeous mountains in the world, including the formidable Matterhorn and the beautiful Mont Blanc.

The Alps have to be the most famous motorcycling region in Europe. Perfectly engineered roads cut through the heart of the mountains, offering challenging, exciting riding alongside breathtaking mountain scenery. Switzerland boasts numerous drivable passes on an unending spiral of perfect tarmac. Italy's Stelvio Pass is hairpin heaven, and Austria is home to the famous, mighty Grossglockner Pass, a not-to-be-missed motorcycle experience. There are bike-friendly hotels and welcoming restaurants throughout this region.

The Route

The following route can easily be ridden in four days and is just a tantalizing taste of the thrilling riding you can expect in the Alps.

Start with a fairly short day's ride of about 125 miles (200 km). From Zürich, head south via the lovely Lake Lucerne towards the mountain resort of Meiringen. Pull over and enjoy excellent Alpine views over lunch before the afternoon fun begins. First is the dramatic Grimsel Pass at 7,103 feet (2,165 m), followed closely by the 7,975-foot (2,431-m) climb over the Furka Pass with its fabulous views of the Rhône Glacier. This is a ride of multiple switchbacks and knuckle-whitening hairpins that carve through the mountains on a thrilling serpentine road, guaranteed to get the adrenaline going and your gearbox working overtime.

above: Zernez and the Swiss National Park.

above: Climbing the Timmelsjoch Pass.

below: Riding through the Alps.

Descend the pass and ride into the town of Andermatt. Surrounded by mountains, it is a popular stopover with motorcyclists, so park for the night, talk bikes, and share a beer with other riders.

Clock up about 186 miles (300 km) as you leave Andermatt and head south over the famous St. Gotthard Pass. Snake through the mountains on some of the finest roads you can ride. Pass through the lovely old town of Bellinzona, climb up and over the 6,768-foot (2,063-m) San Bernardino Pass, then head east onto the hairpins of the Splügen Pass, which passes over the Swiss/Italian border to the lovely town of Chiavenna. Wines, meats, and cheeses matured in the rocks surrounding the town are a local specialty. Park at one of the outdoor cafés and enjoy panoramic views and regional fare while your engine cools before the afternoon's ride. Cross back into Switzerland and ride past the forests, lakes, and snow-capped peaks of the breathtakingly beautiful Engadine Valley. Splurge and spend a night at the glitzy resort of St. Moritz, or continue 21 miles (35 km) north to the peaceful little town of Zernez, close to the alpine wilderness of the Swiss National Park.

From Zernez, head southeast for about 62 miles (100 km) over the Italian border. Ride towards the spa town of Merano. The Timmelsjoch Pass, at 8,231 feet (2,509 m), is possibly Austria's most famous pass after the Grossglockner, and a must for any motorcyclists heading to this region of the Alps. The succession of hairpin bends on excellent tarmac are a joy to ride as the road leads you high into the scenic peaks. Roll down from the pass and spend the night in lively Innsbruck, the capital of Austria's Tyrol. Get some rest before the ride of your life the next day on the 12,460-feet (3,798-m) Grossglockner Pass.

From Innsbruck, it is about a two-and-a-half-hour ride to Bruck/Fusch and the start of the Grossglockner. This pass extends a very warm welcome to riders, with information, parking, and free lockers provided along the way. At the 8,500-foot (2,571-m) Edelweiss Peak, there is an exclusive motorcycle meeting and information point with reserved bike parking (no coaches) and a "bikers' nest" where you can view the history of the road from a biker's perspective. The motorcyclists' day ticket to the Grossglockner also includes entry to the Gerlos and Nockalm roads in the same season, and the option of a reduced ticket for the Villach Alpine Road. The ticket includes free admission to the exhibition and information centers strung along the road. This, combined with the scattering of restaurants perched at vantage points throughout the route, and the numerous viewpoints offering breathtaking panoramas and photographic opportunities, makes this a must ride for bikers heading to the Alps. You can almost reach out and touch the peaks as you negotiate an amazing 39 hairpins over 30 miles (48 km). Perfect your cornering on the sweeping, smooth asphalt and grin from ear to ear as you hone your riding skills on a continuing parade of fabulous mountainous hairpins. Leave the Grossglockner and head to the café-filled square of Lienz, a picturesque town close to the Italian border, over which the rose-tinted pinnacles of the Dolomites await.

The dramatic Grimsel Pass.

Bike: It is possible to take your own bike into Switzerland. Bike hire is available in Zürich. There are operators offering bike-inclusive tours.

Weather Watch: Most passes are open from June until October. The main high passes have a website, so check weather conditions before setting out. Traffic is at its heaviest from late July to late August.

Extending the Ride: From Lienz take a short ride southwest to Cortina d'Ampezzo in the Italian Dolomites or cross into Slovenia over the Wurzen Pass.

The sweeping roads of the Dolomites.

ITALY

THE DOLOMITES

Ride the fabled Great Dolomites Road from Bolzano through the heart of the Dolomites to Cortina d'Ampezzo.

Located in northern Italy, the Dolomites are dramatic, jagged, rocky pinnacles that rise high above forested valleys filled with wildflowers and emerald lakes. The high altitude peaks of the Dolomites were added to UNESCO's World Natural Heritage List in 2009. Cable cars allow you to access walking trails that are more than 1 mile (2,000 m) long, where you can enjoy easy walking between refuges serving traditional fare and excellent wine.

The road surfaces are generally very good, but these are mountain passes, so expect the occasional unpaved stretch. Check the regional tourist board websites for updates on the opening and closing of the passes. Avoid traveling in August, when most of Italy takes a vacation and buses from all over Europe block the narrow roads. There are very few straight roads in the Dolomites. Sheer, vertical rock faces tower above tarmac that hugs the base of the mountains. The surrounding views are stunning, making it difficult to keep your eyes on the road, but it is definitely the warm Italian welcome that makes motorcycling in this region so special. The mountain passes link the picturesque valleys, where almost every hotel or restaurant will have signs proclaiming, "Bikers Welcome" and offering special "Biker Menus." Hotels often display an orange sign with a motorcycle logo proclaiming *moto sotto il tetto* (bike under the roof), and often offer secure parking, touring information, and spa facilities designed to ease your limbs after a long day's ride. Make the most of the fantastic hospitality and get yourself a base for a few days. Unpack your kit, meet other riders staying at the hotel, and watch the towering peaks turn rose pink at sunset as you plan the next day's ride from the comfort of the hotel bar.

above: Cortina d'Ampezzo.

The Sella mountain group, part of the Dolomites.

The Route

This is a classic riding route, combined with side trips on roads that wind over fabulous passes and past vertical rock faces. The 62-mile (100-km) ride from Bolzano to Cortina d'Ampezzo can easily be covered in a day, but it's recommended you spend at least one night in the Dolomites to explore the surrounding passes.

Start in the beautiful old town of Bolzano, the capital of Trentino-Alto Adige/South Tyrol in northern Italy. Head southeast on the Great Dolomites Road (SS241) toward Carezza Lake, where the jagged spires of the Latemar and Catinaccio chains reflect in the lake's tranquil, turquoise waters. From Carezza, the road climbs the Costalunga Pass. The village of Vigo di Fassa sits on a plateau, surrounded by mountains. Its location and the choice of hotels and restaurants make this a good base for exploring the roads in the Catinaccio/Rosengarten range.

Leaving the village, the wooded road curls down into the Fassa Valley and onto the lively resort of Canazei, another good base for exploring the area, especially if you intend to ride around the Sella mountain group. This fabulous loop of passes is a delight to ride—the road must have been designed by a motorcyclist. Once you've ridden the loop—possibly a few times—rejoin the Great Dolomites Road (SS48).

The Pordoi Pass (7,349 feet/2,240 m) marks the border between South Tyrol and the province of Veneto. This is a fantastic

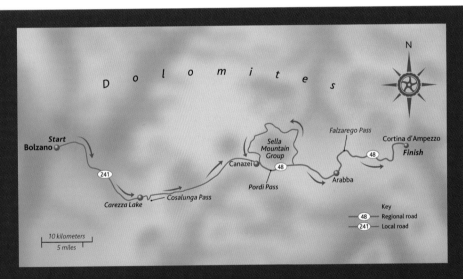

Bike: It is possible to take your own bike into Italy. Bike hire is available in Venice, Verona, and other major cities. There are operators offering bike-inclusive tours and hotels offering guided routes.

Weather Watch: June to early October is the best time to visit. August is crowded and best avoided.

Extending the Ride: From Cortina d'Ampezzo, cross the border into Austria or Slovenia.

ride of about 8 miles (13 km) of switchbacks. At the summit of Pordoi, pull over for a breathtaking panorama of the Dolomites massif. There are cafés and places to snack at the pass, or you can stay at one of the biker-friendly hotels and take a walk into the mountains. The pass leads to the town of Arabba, a popular stopping spot for bikers. Ease off the throttle as you ride through a number of small towns before the road climbs up over the Falzarego Pass.

Through a series of smooth curves and bends, the road descends to the lively town of Cortina d'Ampezzo, which is surrounded by some of the most magnificent mountains of the Dolomite range. Relax with a cool drink in the town square as you watch the stream of motorcycles thundering down from the passes. Quite simply *molto-bellissimo*!

above: Carezza Lake.

below: Although beautiful in winter, the Dolomites are best visited in warmer months on a bike.

Lake Bled.

SLOVENIA/ CROATIA

THE JULIAN ALPS TO THE OPATIJA RIVIERA

This route takes in medieval towns and cities, karst landscapes, and the mountains of Triglav National Park, ending on the Istria Peninsula in Croatia.

Nestled between the Alps and the Adriatic Sea, Slovenia is one of Europe's smallest and loveliest countries. At the heart of Europe, this little-known country of wild, ancient forests and glacial lakes is the perfect antidote to the summer crowds. The limestone peaks and green valleys in the northwest are the most southerly extension of the great alpine range, which sweeps across from neighboring Austria and Italy. To the south, quiet roads weave toward the warm waters of the Adriatic.

At barely 186 miles (300 km) wide, Slovenia may be small, but it has big landscapes. Rural towns and villages provide inexpensive accommodation and a friendly welcome, and there is a relaxed feel to a journey in this beautiful, peaceful country. Road surfaces are generally very good, although some of the small back roads can be a little rough. Traffic is much lighter this side of the Alps, and you will find yourself riding on empty roads that lead over vine-covered hills into forested valleys and high over alpine passes.

The Route

The following route should take a few days, but allow a little longer if you want to explore the national parks.

From the pretty medieval town of Cividale del Friuli in northern Italy, cross the border into Slovenia's Soca Valley, named after the powerful waters of the Soca River. The road meanders through densely wooded hills toward the town of Kobarid. The short 14-mile (23-km) ride from Kobarid to Bovec on the 102 is on a scenic road that follows the emerald waters of the Soca. The

above: Pausing for lunch in a town square in Slovenia.

Vrsic Pass.

little town of Bovec sits on the edge of Triglav National Park, named after the country's highest mountain, Triglav (9,396 feet/2,864 m). The park's terrain, forests, peaks, and valleys offer countless outdoor activity opportunities.

Leaving Bovec, ride out onto the 206 heading northeast and onto the village of Trenta. From Trenta, the road starts to climb steeply toward the 5,285-foot (1,611-m) summit of the Vrsic Pass, the highest mountain pass in Slovenia and a highlight of any motorcycle trip to Slovenia. The Vrsic Pass stretches for just 15 miles (25 km) between Trenta and Kranjska Gora. The road curls up toward the summit through a steep wooded valley. The road's 50 hairpin bends (26 on the Trenta side and 24 on the Kranjska Gora side) are all numbered and the altitude recorded. Approaching the pass from Trenta, the road is narrow but wide enough for two-lane traffic and in reasonable condition. Magnificent snow-capped peaks surround the summit, where there is parking and a large mountain hut that has a shop and serves refreshments. Heading down toward Kranjska Gora, the road is partially cobbled and almost single-track. As the road winds slowly down and on to the flat, you come to Lake Jasna, a large artificial lake with the Julian Alps as its backdrop. It is then just a few miles to Kranjska Gora, Slovenia's main ski resort.

From Kranjska Gora, take the 201. The wide road sweeps below steep hills and white peaks, affording great views as you ride about 24 miles (40 km) toward Lake Bled, one of Slovenia's most photographed landmarks. Restaurants and shops line the lakeshore, and you can take a gondola across to Bled Island. Get back on your bike and continue onto the beautiful Lake Bohinj, where the encircling mountains reflect in its tranquil waters.

To reach Ljubljana, when leaving Lake Bohinj, take the steep, narrow 909 toward Zgornja Sorica. On a clear day, the views back to the lake are spectacular. As you drop out of the hills and join the 403, the road runs alongside the

Sora River. From Zelezniki, continue on a mainly flat road through the valley on to Skofja Loka, a small, beautifully preserved medieval city. Ljubljana, Slovenia's capital, lies just 14 miles (22 km) southeast on the 211. The city is small but lively, so park your bike at a free motorcycle parking area and relax in one of the many restaurants, bars, or cafés in the area.

From Ljubljana, head south for about 31 miles (50 km) to Postojna, the closest town for visiting the huge chambers of the Postojna Caves and the medieval Predjama Castle. From here it is a short ride to the Skocjan Caves, a UNESCO world heritage site and one of Slovenia's most stunning natural attractions. From Postojna, head south to Jelsane to cross into Croatia at Rupa and onto the resort of Opatija on the Adriatic. The former Habsburg royal palaces and villas line the 7-mile (12-km) promenade. Find yourself a palace-turned-luxury-hotel and take a ride around the Istria Peninsula.

above left: A cobbled section of Vrsic Pass.

above right: Triglav National Park.

Bike: It is possible to take your own bike into Slovenia and Croatia. Bike hire is available in Ljubljana. There are operators offering bike-inclusive tours.

Weather Watch: May to September is the best time to visit.

Extending the Ride: Continue into Croatia, or cross into Italy and head to the Italian Dolomites.

Cappadocia's volcanic landscape.

TURKEY

ISTANBUL LOOP VIA ANATOLIA AND THE COAST

From Istanbul, cross the Sea of Marmara and head east to the lunar landscapes of central Anatolia, through the Taurus Mountains, and along the Turquoise Coast. Finally, head north along the Aegean coast, returning to Istanbul via the Dardanelles.

This is a country steeped in layers of history and legend. Ruins of the Roman and Byzantine empires lie scattered along the Mediterranean and Aegean coasts, and Cappadocia's troglodyte Christian churches and lunar landscape enthrall visitors to central Anatolia. You can also watch the Whirling Dervishes of Konya and discover the ancient city of Troy.

The warmth and friendliness of the Turkish people make a motorcycle journey through Turkey a rewarding and pleasurable experience. Stopping to ask the way often results in a place at the *tavla* (backgammon) table, drinks on the house, or an invitation to meet friends and family. The hospitality is genuine and gracious and will accompany you from the metropolis of Istanbul all throughout the coastal towns and sleepy villages. Turkish hospitality is matched by its delicious and varied cuisine. Even on the quietest of back roads, you are never far from a restaurant or café—often the hub of the village and an ideal place to meet people.

For the Turkish people, motorcycling as a hobby is a relatively new phenomenon, and you are more likely now to meet Turkish riders discovering their country by motorcycle than ever before. Road conditions vary from smooth, fast highways—linking the main cities—to bumpy rural roads. Major roads are not regularly maintained and can quickly switch from perfect to potholed tarmac, but the pace is never fast and the distances between towns never huge. Once discovered, lunch at a *lokanta* (restaurant) will become a daily highlight of your day's ride, and you will quickly get into a relaxed riding pace.

above: Posing for the camera in Turkey.

The Route

Turkey is a huge and vastly varied country offering endless motorcycling possibilities. If you have two weeks, try the following leisurely 1,864-mile (3,000-km) loop from Istanbul.

Istanbul has to be one of the most beautiful cities in the world, so linger a few days to appreciate its many charms. Riding through Istanbul's densely packed ancient streets is hair-raising, but someone will always point you in the right direction. Once out on the open road, the pace is leisurely and traffic is generally light. It will take about an hour to ride out of the city to the ferry terminal at Eskihisar for a 30-minute crossing of the Sea of Marmara to Topcular, or, if you wish to avoid riding in the city traffic, you can cross from Yenikapı in the old city to Yalova or Bandırma. Rolling off the ferry, you will have a straight ride on lovely mountain roads that wind for 112 miles (180 km) via the eastern tip of Lake İznik to Bursa, nestled in the lower slopes of Uludag Mountain. Famous as the first capital of the Ottoman Empire, it also has a well-deserved reputation for its delicious İskender kebab and *kestane sekeri*, a chestnut-based candy. Spend the evening wandering the bazaars buying local delicacies to store in your tank bag.

Heading northeast, the road to Safranbolu follows valleys, lakes, and mountains (via Bozüyük and Bolu) for almost 280 miles (450 km). Picnic on the treats you bought at the bazaars as you stop to enjoy the views. Safranbolu is a beautifully preserved Ottoman town, and also a UNESCO World Heritage Site. Soak in 17th-century baths and spend the night in a restored Ottoman house.

It is a full day's ride to the unique landscape of the central Anatolian plateau. The road winds through the beautiful mountain passes of the western Black Sea Mountains, dropping on to the volcanic landscapes of Cappadocia.

Swapping saddles.

Grand Bazaar, Istanbul.

Ride through valleys of strangely eroded rock formations to cave churches adorned with frescos and underground cities carved in the soft volcanic rock. Accommodation options in Göreme and Ürgüp are plentiful and varied. Stay in a cave hotel—lovely and cool during the day, their vantage points often command the most fantastic views of the ever-changing colors of the rock. Watch the sun set on this mysterious moonscape as you sip the local wine, which has been produced in this region for centuries.

It is a fast ride west for 186 miles (300 km) through the agricultural flatlands of central Turkey to Konya, spiritual home of the mystical sect of the Whirling Dervishes and a city famous throughout the Muslim world. Departing Konya, it is a great day's ride across the Taurus Mountains to the Mediterranean Sea. Take the secondary road via Beysehir to Antalya, and you will be rewarded with a fantastic 75-mile (120-km) ride and stunning views. The city of Antalya is the gateway to the resorts of the Mediterranean, so if you want to kick off your boots for a few days, the coastal route is lined with sandy beaches, archaeological sites, and innumerable places to stay. If you only visit one Greco-Roman site, it has to be Ephesus, 249 miles (400 km) from Antalya, just outside the town of Selcuk along the Aegean coast. Beautifully preserved, it is easy to spend a day wandering amongst the temples, theaters, and baths. It's a huge site and definitely not to be tackled in the heat of the day wearing full leathers!

As you ride north along the Aegean coast, stop to visit the legendary site of Troy, lying just 12 miles (20 km) south of Canakkale. There are regular ferries from Canakkale across the Dardanelles to the Gallipoli peninsula, the scene of terrible fighting during WWI, and now a national park. From here, it is just a few hours' ride back to Istanbul. Barter in the Grand Bazaar, marvel at the opulence of the Ottoman Empire, and admire the beautiful skyline on an evening cruise along the Bosphorus.

Bike: It is possible to take your own bike into Turkey. Bike hire is available in Istanbul and Ankara. There are operators offering bike-inclusive tours.

Weather Watch: Daytime temperatures are pleasant in early May and mid-September. June to August is very hot and the crowds increase along the coast at this time.

Extending the Ride: No overland connection to other featured journeys.

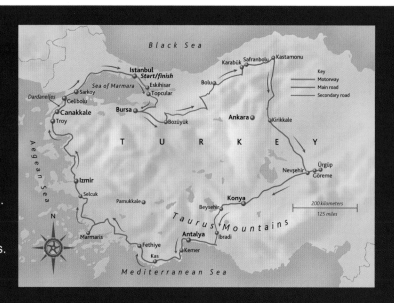

INDEX

Africa
Kenya (Nairobi to Central Highlands and Great Rift Valley), 23–25
Morocco (Ceuta to Marrakech Loop), 17–21
Namibia (Windhoek to Etosha National Park), 29–31
South Africa (Cape Town Circuit through Garden Route), 33–37
Alice Springs, Darwin to (Australia), 131–33
Alps/Alpes, 183. See also France; Slovenia/Croatia; Switzerland/Austria
Anchorage, Alaska (USA) to Whitehorse Loop (Canada), 53–57
Andalucía, circuit of (Spain), 185–87
Annecy circuit via Côte d'Azur (France), 177–79
Argentina/Chile (Patagonia: Journey to end of the world), 87–91
Asia. See also India
Mongolia (Ulaanbaatar to Gobi Desert Loop), 125–27
Sri Lanka (Colombo Circuit), 101–5
Thailand (Chiang Mai to Golden Triangle Loop), 117–19
Vietnam (circuit north from Hanoi), 121–23
Australia. See also New Zealand
Darwin to Alice Springs, 131–33
Great Ocean Road, 139–41
Oodnadatta Track, 135–37
Austria (Swiss Alps to Austrian Tyrol), 189–91

Baja Peninsula, Sierra Madres Mountains to (Mexico), 81–85
Bilbao to Perpignan Loop (France/Spain), 181–83
Black Hills, Denver to Durango via (USA), 63–67
Boston to Green Mountains (USA), 59–61

Calgary to Jasper National Park (Canada), 41–43
California
Route 66: Flagstaff to Los Angeles, 77–79
Wild West and Californian coast, 71–75
Canada
Anchorage, Alaska (USA) to Whitehorse Loop, 53–57
Gulf of Maine to Strait of Belle Isle, 49–51
Montréal to Gaspé Peninsula, 45–47
the Rockies: Calgary to Jasper National Park, 41–43
Cape Town Circuit through Garden Route (South Africa), 33–37
Central Highlands to Great Rift Valley, Nairobi to (Kenya), 23–25
Ceuta to Marrakech Loop (Morocco), 17–21
Chiang Mai to Golden Triangle Loop (Thailand), 117–19
Chile/Argentina (Patagonia: Journey to end of the world), 87–91
Cliffs of Moher, Cork to (Ireland), 163–65
Colombo Circuit (Sri Lanka), 101–5
Colorado (Denver to Durango via Black Hills), 63–67
Cordillera de Guanacaste, San José to (Costa Rica), 87–91
Cork to Cliffs of Moher (Ireland), 163–65
Costa Rica (San José to Cordillera de Guanacaste), 87–91
Côte d'Azur, Annecy circuit via (France), 177–79
Croatia/Slovenia (Julian Alps to Opatija Riviera), 197–99

Darwin to Alice Springs (Australia), 131–33
Delhi to Jaisalmer (India), 107–11
Denver to Durango via Black Hills (USA), 63–67
Dolomites (Italy), 193–95

east coast (USA), Boston to Green Mountains, 59–61
Edinburgh to Gairloch (Scotland), 157–61
England (Kendal to Whitby), 167–71
Etosha National Park, Windhoek to (Namibia), 29–31
Europe
England (Kendal to Whitby), 167–71
France (Annecy circuit via Côte d'Azur), 177–79
Germany (Rhineland and Nürburgring), 173–75
Iceland (Ring Road tour), 149–51
Ireland (Cork to Cliffs of Moher), 163–65
Italy (Dolomites), 193–95
Norway (Fjordland to North Cape), 153–55
Scotland (Edinburgh to Gairloch), 157–61
Slovenia/Croatia (Julian Alps to Opatija Riviera), 197–99
Spain (circuit of Andalucía), 185–87
Spain/France (Bilbao to Perpignan Loop), 181–83
Switzerland/Austria (Swiss Alps to Austrian Tyrol), 189–91
Turkey (Istanbul Loop via Anatolia/coast), 201–5

Fjordland to North Cape (Norway), 153–55
Flagstaff to Los Angeles (Route 66), 77–79
France (Annecy circuit via Côte d'Azur), 177–79
France/Spain (Bilbao to Perpignan Loop), 181–83

Gairloch, Edinburgh to (Scotland), 157–61
Garden Route, Cape Town Circuit through (South Africa), 33–37
Gaspé Peninsula, Montréal to (Canada), 45–47
Germany (Rhineland and Nürburgring), 173–75
Gobi Desert Loop, Ulaanbaatar to (Mongolia), 125–27
Golden Triangle Loop, Chiang Mai to (Thailand), 117–19
Great Ocean Road (Australia), 139–41
Great Rift Valley, Nairobi to Central Highlands and (Kenya), 23–25
Green Mountains, Boston to (USA), 59–61
Gulf of Maine to Strait of Belle Isle (Canada), 49–51

Hanoi, circuit north from (Vietnam), 121–23

Iceland (Ring Road tour), 149–51
India
Delhi to Jaisalmer, 107–11
Manali to Leh, 113–15
Ireland (Cork to Cliffs of Moher), 163–65
Istanbul Loop via Anatolia/coast (Turkey), 201–5
Italy (Dolomites), 193–95

Jaisalmer, Delhi to (India), 107–11
Jasper National Park, Calgary to (Canada), 41–43
Julian Alps to Opatija Riviera (Slovenia/Croatia), 197–99

Kendal to Whitby (England), 167–71

Leh, Manali to (India), 113–15
Los Angeles, Flagstaff to (Route 66), 77–79

Manali to Leh (India), 113–15
Marrakech Loop, Ceuta to (Morocco), 17–21
Mexico (Sierra Madres Mountains to Baja Peninsula), 81–85
Mongolia (Ulaanbaatar to Gobi Desert Loop), 125–27
Montréal to Gaspé Peninsula (Canada), 45–47
Morocco (Ceuta to Marrakech Loop), 17–21
motorcycles
allure of trips on, 7–9
hiring in country, 11

journeys in this book and, 9–11
taking/using your own, 11

Nairobi to Central Highlands and Great Rift Valley (Kenya), 23–25
Namibia (Windhoek to Etosha National Park), 29–31
New Zealand (South Island circuit), 143–45
North Cape, Fjordland to (Norway), 153–55
Norway (Fjordland to North Cape), 153–55
Nova Scotia (Gulf of Maine to Strait of Belle Isle), 49–51

Oodnadatta Track (Australia), 135–37
Opatija Riviera, Julian Alps to (Slovenia/Croatia), 197–99

Patagonia (Chile/Argentina), 87–91
Perpignan Loop, Bilbao to (France/Spain), 181–83
planning trips
hiring vs taking your motorcycle, 11
journeys in this book and, 9–11
perspective on, 4–5
travel requirements, 12

Rhineland and Nürburgring (Germany), 173–75
Ring Road tour (Iceland), 149–51
Rockies: Calgary to Jasper National Park (Canada), 41–43
Rockies: Denver to Durango via Black Hills (USA), 63–67
Route 66: Flagstaff to Los Angeles (USA), 77–79

San José to Cordillera de Guanacaste (Costa Rica), 87–91
Scotland (Edinburgh to Gairloch), 157–61
Sierra Madres Mountains to Baja Peninsula (Mexico), 81–85
Slovenia/Croatia (Julian Alps to Opatija Riviera), 197–99
South Africa (Cape Town Circuit through Garden Route), 33–37
South Dakota (Denver to Durango via Black Hills), 63–67
South Island circuit (New Zealand), 143–45
Spain (circuit of Andalucía), 185–87
Spain/France (Bilbao to Perpignan Loop), 181–83
Sri Lanka (Colombo Circuit), 101–5
Strait of Belle Isle, Gulf of Maine to (Canada), 49–51
Switzerland/Austria (Swiss Alps to Austrian Tyrol), 189–91

Thailand (Chiang Mai to Golden Triangle Loop), 117–19

travel requirements, 12. See also planning trips
Turkey (Istanbul Loop via Anatolia/coast), 201–5

Ulaanbaatar to Gobi Desert Loop (Mongolia), 125–27
USA trips
Anchorage, Alaska (USA) to Whitehorse Loop, 53–57
Boston to Green Mountains, 59–61
Denver to Durango via Black Hills, 63–67
Route 66: Flagstaff to Los Angeles, 77–79
Wild West and Californian coast, 71–75

Vietnam (circuit north from Hanoi), 121–23

Whitby, Kendal to (England), 167–71
Whitehorse Loop (Canada), Anchorage, Alaska (USA) to, 53–57
Wild West and Californian coast (USA), 71–75
Windhoek to Etosha National Park (Namibia), 29–31
wine trails, Rhineland (Germany), 173–75

PHOTO CREDITS

Special thanks to all the tour operators who provided photos for this book: Fredlink Tours & Safari (*www.motorbike-safari.com*), Africa Motion Tours (*www.africamotiontours.com*), Springbok Atlas (*www.springbokatlas.com*), Motorcycle Tour Guide Nova Scotia (*www.motorcycletourguidens.com*), Sha Lanka Tours (*www.negombo-motorcycle-tours.com*), Moto Tours Asia (*www.mototoursasia.com*), Off The Map Tours/Bike Mongolia (*www.bikemongolia.com*), Bike Round Oz (*www.bikeroundoz.com*), MI Motor Tours (*www.motoireland.com*), H-C Travel Ltd (*www.hctravel.com*), Iberian Moto Tours (*www.imtbike.com*), Kazoom Moto Adventures (*www.kazoom-moto-adventures.com*).

ABOUT COLETTE COLEMAN

Motorcycle adventurer Colette Coleman has spent 30 years riding motorcycles over six continents, including an overland ride from the UK to Australia, and still believes the best way to explore the world is on two wheels. Returning from the overland expedition in 1997, she started working in travel, initially creating tours in Russia, Mongolia, China, and Central Asia. Colette spent many years working for several of the UK's leading action and adventure tour operators, developing and operating adventure tours across the globe. She has written two motorcycle touring books, *Magnificent Motorcycle Trips of the World* (originally published as *Great Motorcycle Journeys of the World* [New Holland 2008]) and *Great Motorcycle Tours of Europe* (Quercus 2014), which have been translated into four languages. Colette has written numerous articles for the travel and motorcycle press, including contributions to the first 1997 edition of the *Adventure Motorcycle Handbook* (Trailblazer). Colette now combines travel writing with running her own travel agency specializing in adventure holidays, including self-guided motorcycle tours. She lives in the Yorkshire Dales with her husband, Steve, and continues to travel at every opportunity. Visit her at *www.colettecoleman.com*.

ACKNOWLEDGMENTS

To my husband, mechanic, and riding companion, Steve, who remembered the roads I had long forgotten. Thanks to good friends Ian Freeman and Lee Prescott—their contribution and loan of images, based on their own extensive motorcycle touring, was invaluable and much appreciated.

Magnificent Motorcycle Trips of the World

CompanionHouse Books™ is an imprint of Fox Chapel Publishers International Ltd.

Project Team
Vice President—Content: Christopher Reggio
Editors: Colleen Dorsey and Katie Ocasio
Art Director: Mary Ann Kahn
Designer: David Fisk
Index: Jay Kreider

978-1-62008-238-6

The Cataloging-in-Publication Data is on file with the Library of Congress.

This book has been published with the intent to provide accurate and authoritative information in regard to the subject matter within. While every precaution has been taken in the preparation of this book, the author and publisher expressly disclaim any responsibility for any errors, omissions, or adverse effects arising from the use or application of the information contained herein.

We are always looking for talented authors. To submit an idea, please send a brief inquiry to acquisitions@foxchapelpublishing.com.

CompanionHouse Books
903 Square Street, Mount Joy, PA 17552
www.facebook.com/companionhousebooks

Fox Chapel Publishers International Ltd.
7 Danefield Road, Selsey (Chichester)
West Sussex PO20 9DA, U.K.

Printed and bound in Singapore
20 19 18 17   2 4 6 8 10 9 7 5 3 1